AUSTRALIA'S
HOME BUYING
GUIDE

HOW TO BUY A PROPERTY
FASTER AND FOR LESS

TODD SLOAN

First published in 2021 by Major Street Publishing Pty Ltd
E | info@majorstreet.com.au W | majorstreet.com.au M | +61 421 707 983

A catalogue record for this book is available from
the National Library of Australia

NATIONAL
LIBRARY
OF AUSTRALIA

Printed book ISBN: 978-0-6489804-9-0
Ebook ISBN: 978-1-9226110-0-0

Cover design by Tess McCabe
Cover image by Bianca Princic
Internal design by Production Works
Printed in Australia by Ovato, an Accredited ISO AS/NZS 14001:2004
Environmental Management System Printer.

10 9 8 7 6 5 4 3 2 1

CONTENTS

PREFACE

I wrote this book for two reasons: one's altruistic, and the other's a little more selfish. First, the altruistic reason: I genuinely have a passion for helping people and making a sometimes scary or stressful process accessible and fun. I speak with literally hundreds of people every week about buying and selling property, and I can say with 100 per cent honesty I try my best to help every single one of them. It really is a fantastic feeling when someone drops into the office with a big smile and a bottle of wine in hand and says, 'Your tips saved us so much money. Thank you!' (Just to be clear, they don't walk in drunk saying this; the wine is a gift.)

I will continue to help people buy and sell property for as long as I can. The only issue is that I can only be in one place at a time. When I sit down with a client, I am 100 per cent in the room, giving them my complete and undivided attention. This is precisely what I should be doing; but it means that I can only help a limited number of people.

I needed a better way of supporting people at any time and in any place, when it's convenient for them. From this, the idea for this book was born. I have worked on this book for two years in three different countries, writing it whenever a helpful idea came to mind and I had a moment to spare. I've been known to interrupt my own gym workout to jot down ideas for a chapter as soon as they came to mind. I tell you this because I want you to know this book has been a complete labour of love, driven by my overwhelming desire to help people get to where they want to go.

This book is a collection of learnings from my 12-plus years of real estate experience. You'll learn from the mistakes I made buying my first property at 21, as well as deals I've put together in more recent years. By making a choice to read this book, you're giving yourself a massive competitive edge over all the other buyers in the marketplace. This book was written specifically for the current Australian housing market, and its aim is to get you into your first or next home faster and for less. Reading this book will potentially save you thousands of dollars.

And now for the selfish reason I wrote this book. Growing up as a dyslexic kid in the public school system was not a very fun experience. I think it's going to feel pretty cool to say I've written a book – and to send a copy to my high school English teacher who told me I was never going to achieve anything. It's my rockstar drop-the-mic moment.

Happy reading, and even happier house hunting!

Todd Sloan
info@pizzaandproperty.com

Pizza & Property
podcast•••

My podcast and YouTube channel, Pizza and Property, is packed with videos and podcasts designed to help anyone interested in buying, selling or investing in property. If you're anything like me and sometimes need a break from reading to watch a video or listen to something instead, you're in luck. Sit back in your comfy chair and get ready to digest some in-depth property hints and tips.

pizzaandproperty.com

GETTING STARTED

The secret of getting ahead is getting started.
MARK TWAIN

So you want to buy a property? Congratulations! You're about to take the exciting leap into home ownership. Whether you're buying your first home or moving to a new home for the next chapter of your life, and whether you're buying a brand-new apartment or a heritage-listed character home, the process can seem both exciting and a little scary.

Australia's Home Buying Guide intends to make the process of buying your home simple, breaking it down into manageable and understandable steps. You can work your way through the process with confidence and feel comfortable with each action you take as you get closer to owning your property.

Ever since I can remember, I've loved real estate. If I think back hard enough, it probably stems from my childhood addiction to building houses out of Lego. I would spend hours upon hours building entire suburbs, fascinated with how I could make my little Lego people have the perfect life in my made-up towns.

Now, as an adult, having spent so much of my life researching markets around the country and even in other parts of the world, I have a solid understanding of the best ways to buy and sell properties.

However, it wasn't always like this. When I made my very first purchase over a decade ago, I was so nervous making my way through the process. I know I've made many mistakes over the years. However, I have learnt from all of these mistakes, and I want to make sure I can help you steer clear of the same costly errors I made – in other words, save you a lot of time and money.

After accumulating more than 12 years' experience and with tens of millions of dollars of property transactions behind me, I'm now finally in a position to break down an otherwise intimidating subject and turn it into something more simple – a guide that anyone will feel comfortable following.

Common mistakes to avoid

Throughout this book, I'll share the most common pitfalls and traps you should watch out for when you're at the start of your property search. I'll take you through:

- how to make sure you get your finance approved correctly
- how to make sure you get the best deal on your loan and potentially save thousands of dollars
- how to find the right area for you and your family
- the questions to ask the agent to give you a competitive edge
- how to notice a selling agent's tricks and potentially save stacks of cash
- knowing your rights on cooling off and how they change in each state and territory.

I'll also provide some helpful tips on how to avoid some everyday, costly situations I see buyers fall into all too often.

Helpful tricks and tips to save you time and money

As well as sharing the tips and tricks professionals use, I'll break down the financial jargon and misconceptions you're likely to come across in your search. I'll answer the questions I hear all the time from buyers, such as:

- What's lenders mortgage insurance (LMI), and who does it protect?
- What's a loan-to-value ratio (LVR), and should it be high or low?
- How large a deposit do I need to put down on a property?
- Do I need any savings other than my deposit?

I know this might seem like lots of information to take in, but I promise I have put in every effort to make sure it's as simple as possible to follow. Just keep reading, and you'll discover that the more you read, the more focus and clarity the picture will have.

First, I'll get you feeling comfortable with the financial side of buying a property: budgeting, finding out how much you can borrow and how your loan is going to work for you. Then, it's time to move on to finding the best property for your wants and needs.

There are so many choices when it comes to buying a property, and if you've started talking with family and friends about your intentions to make a purchase, I'm sure everyone has given you their opinion on what they think you should buy. Sometimes, it can be beneficial speaking with friends and family. However, be aware that it can lead to information overload, which can make you feel more lost than when you started. It's not that the people you speak with are trying to make things hard for you – quite the opposite. Most of the time, people give their advice based on what they experienced the last time they bought a property, and tell you what has worked for them. This advice can sometimes be sound if the friend or family member has a lot of experience and has stayed in touch with the market. More often than not, though, it is well-intentioned but very outdated information that moves you away from where you want to be. We're going to talk about how to be careful with cousin Barry and his advice.

Three steps to buying your home

I'm a big believer in breaking things down into simple steps. This approach should help you get to the core of what's truly important: meeting your lifestyle and financial goals. That's why I've written this book in the following three sections:

1. Building the foundation
2. Finding the one
3. Making it yours.

Building the foundation

Deciding where you want to buy your property will come down to budget for most of us. This is probably the first and hardest lesson first home buyers will learn. As much as I want to live in the $100.5 million penthouse of One57 in New York City, I'd have to sell a few more books and houses before that's my reality. I'm all for having big dreams and goals, but in this case, keeping it realistic is critical.

Back to reality – where the view is a little different than from the One57 penthouse – you're going to find out how a good mortgage broker can help you work out what you can afford. Then I'll help you with your budgeting, making a few suggestions on how to increase the chances of achieving your financial goals. Before we have all of the borrowings and budgeting wrapped up, there's one last part to check for you: whether you're entitled to any free money! Even if you think there's no way you're able to qualify for the First Home Owner Grant, I suggest reading this chapter just in case there is a different government scheme that offers you money you may have otherwise missed out on.

Finding the one

You'll find out early on in your property search, on your way to finding 'the one', that the road is bumpy and not always straight.

The process of uncovering things that you may not have thought were important can be extremely valuable. As an agent, I've seen people buy property thinking it's perfect for them, only to find out six months later that the commute to work took away too much of their family time at home; they then had to sell and purchase another property that better suited their needs.

Buying this way will mean you'll incur all kinds of extra costs that could have been avoided if you'd simply taken a few simple steps to figure out what you want, need and won't put up with. It's like an old builder's saying I was told years ago: 'Measure twice, cut once.'

Take a little more time to choose the right home and area in the beginning, because you can't uncut a piece of wood – and it can be very costly to buy another one.

Buying an apartment in a high-rise can give you a fantastic lifestyle. I know this for a fact, as the first property I purchased was in a hotel that had a spa, sauna, pool and gym. It was a great way to live, but there were so many things I didn't know about strata and community title. I want to share those potential pitfalls with you so you can make an educated decision on what you're buying into, not a blind one. Chapter 5 covers all the dos and don'ts of buying into the apartment market.

The final chapter in part II looks at open homes and sorting out the stuff from the fluff.

Making it yours

Once you've built the foundation and found the one, it's time to get into my favourite part: making it yours. Here we look at making offers and negotiating. I'll cover this topic in a simple and straight-forward way designed to give you a strong feeling of confidence when it comes time to make an offer on your new property.

One of my main goals in this section of the book is to break down a lot of the negative stereotypes that people may have about negotiating property deals and making an offer to a selling agent. When I'm dealing with first home buyers, I usually discover that they fit into one of two categories:

1. They're too nervous about negotiating and just accept any terms the agent gives without question.

2. They have a very brutish and arrogant approach, trying to push and assert dominance – thinking, 'I must be tough to get a good deal.'

In reality, once you go through the steps in the first two parts of the book, you should feel confident about what you're buying and how much it's worth. When you have a real understanding of the situation, the negotiation will generally become a much easier process – where both parties express their wants and concerns and work towards a mutual agreement that benefits everyone involved.

I feel there's a misconception that business negotiations have to be confrontational and aggressive, which could not be further from the truth. A former boss of mine always used to say to me, 'You will catch a lot more bees with honey than you will with vinegar.' This was ironic, not only because he was misquoting – I'm pretty sure it's supposed to be flies, not bees – but because he was such an ass to everyone. Whether he took his own advice or not isn't the point. The point is, when you're trying to get what you want, you have a much better chance of getting it when you're going about it politely and confidently.

After you've finalised the negotiation, the next step is cooling off and understanding your legal rights when buying a property. Whether it's your first property purchase or your fiftieth, this last step never becomes any more fun or any less critical.

After reading through this last part of the book, you should feel comfortable with everything you need to know, including:

- how to make your offer as attractive as possible
- how the auction process works, and what you need to be ready for if the property you want to buy is going to auction
- how cooling off works in the state you're buying in
- how to make your settlement flow smoothly and be hassle-free.

How to read this book

You can sit down and read this book all in one go; I've kept it short so you should be able read it in a couple of sittings. However, I've explicitly designed it so that you can read relevant chapters on the go and take the book with you when you're out looking at houses, researching finance and talking to agents. You can keep it in your car, handbag, man bag or whatever you want to carry it in. It's designed to help you get that sense of satisfaction as you tick off the steps in the process and feel yourself getting closer to buying that all-important first home, or next home. All chapters include a summary that reinforces the key takeaway points I feel are most important to remember.

I'm here to help

If you feel overwhelmed or confused at any stage while reading this book, please feel free to send me an email for some personal property advice and let me walk you through your individual situation. I really mean it; if at any point you get stuck, send me an email or a PM via the Pizza and Property Facebook page. I'll be more than happy to chat with you about whatever part of the process you feel stuck on, helping you get to where you need to go.

Well, without any further ado, let's get you into it.

Don't wait to buy real estate.
Buy real estate, and wait.
ROBERT G ALLEN

PART I

BUILDING THE FOUNDATION

1.

GETTING YOUR FINANCES SORTED

*Bringing together the right information with the
right people will dramatically improve a [person's] ability
to develop and act on ... opportunities.*

BILL GATES

In my professional opinion, sorting out finance is where most homebuyers unknowingly trip themselves up from the very start. I see buyers cause themselves a lot of unnecessary disappointment and pain due to not talking with a good mortgage broker at the very beginning. Gone are the days when you approach a bank directly for your home loan. A broker will source the best home loan for you.

Wait, Todd – thanks for your thoughts, but my sister's brother-in-law's cousin's dog works at a bank, and she said they could look after me, so I think I'll skip this chapter...

If you have a connection in the banking world, that's great! You should definitely talk to them. I don't ever want to discourage you from talking to a friend, family member or anyone else who has been strongly recommended. I'm not saying these people won't look after you; it's just that if you go directly to the bank, how will you know that you're getting the best deal that's out there for you?

Finance definitely isn't the fun part of buying a home, but if you start by shopping for a property before you see a broker, you might be completely wasting your time. You could be shopping in a price range that's way out of your budget, or you could be a lot closer to your dream home than you actually thought. You could have spent a considerable amount of time looking at the wrong kinds of homes instead of searching for the home you'd always dreamed of.

What does a mortgage broker do?

A good broker will break down your financial situation and give you an accurate picture of what you can borrow, how much the weekly, fortnightly, or monthly repayments are going to be and, best of all, can help you get pre-approval.

Pre-approval: when a lender has agreed on an amount that it is most likely willing to lend you based on the details you have provided of your financial situation.

So once you have your pre-approval, *it's time to go shopping for your property!* Yay!

Think of it this way: imagine you need to buy a new phone. You're in a shopping centre and happen to walk into a Telstra shop. You sit down with a good sales rep – we'll call her Jennifer. As you describe your situation, Jennifer is listening to every word you say. You tell her about your needs and wants: everything that's important to you.

Jennifer asks you some questions that help you uncover a few needs you may not have even known you had. She acts with professionalism and care, and offers a depth of knowledge that puts you at ease. When it comes time for you to make your choice out of Jennifer's recommendations, she makes you feel comfortable that she's giving you the best deal she can, and that you're being looked after. The thing is, Jennifer *is* looking after you, but she's looking after you the best way she can – she's not necessarily giving you the best deal that's available to you in the market, only in that store.

In my opinion, the problem with this situation isn't that Jennifer acted with any ill intent, or didn't know what she was doing. This hypothetical sales rep may be the most amazing and knowledgeable salesperson in the whole company. The problem with this situation is that you may have just received the best deal that Telstra has to offer, but how do you know that Vodafone isn't actually a better fit for you? Or maybe Optus is going to give you some extra features for free that Telstra is charging you for. My point is, you don't know.

You don't know if you're getting the best deal that's out there when you meet a sales rep who works exclusively for one company. Of course, they're going to say their product is better than their competitors'. Jennifer won't have her job at Telstra for very long if she says, 'Actually, Harvey Norman sounds like it would suit your needs better; plus, it has a special on at the moment. It's just 50 metres away, on the left. Have a nice day.'

However, that's precisely what a good broker does. They listen to what you need and find the best options from a range of lenders – not just the options from the one lender they work for – and give you the choice of which lender fits your situation the best.

A small saving goes a long way

A small difference in the interest rate on your home loan can some-times make a massive impact on how much money stays in your pocket and how much extra you give to the bank.

Think of it this way: if a broker could save you just 0.5 per cent off your rate, you might think, 'Well, that's okay, but I'm not that fussed about such a small interest rate saving.' But did you know that on a loan of $600,000, the difference of 0.5 per cent off your interest rate could save you $57,000?*

Let's have a think about what you could buy with $57,000. At the time of writing this chapter in 2021, $57,000 will buy you a six-month-long trip to Europe in four-star accommodation (as soon as COVID travel restrictions are relaxed). Or, if holidays aren't your thing, how about a 2020 Mercedes Benz A or B class? I've just found 100 of them for sale online, each under $57,000.

If holidays and fancy cars don't get you going, then how about eating your way into a fancy food coma, going out to dinner at a beautiful restaurant every night of the week for one whole year? You could spend $156 every night experiencing culinary heaven and avoid doing any dinner dishes for an entire year! That sounds amazing to me. Personally, I think I'd be boring and use $45,000 on a deposit for an investment property and go on an excellent little $12,000 holiday to France (once international borders reopen!).

To be clear, I'm not recommending you spend your money on any of these things (apart from the investment property – go to town on them). All I'm saying is that having the extra money in your life to do these fun and awesome things is not attached to winning a lot-tery ticket; you can achieve this via simple due diligence and making sure you choose the right home loan for your situation. In other words, while your sister's brother-in-law's cousin's dog working for

---

* The savings figure generated is based on a $600,000 principal and interest loan over 30 years, varying the original interest rate from 3.0 per cent to 2.5 per cent.

the bank may have the best product for you, if they don't you may be giving away a fancy car, trips around the world and lots of other fun life experiences that belong to you.

Due diligence: the investigation that a reasonable person is expected to take before entering into an agreement or contract.

A broker has access to many lenders, all with different criteria and all looking for different kinds of customers for their 'loan book'. Having the right broker on your side gives you an unbiased opinion on what could be the best deal for you based on the answers you have given them.

Who pays the broker?

You may be wondering, why does a broker provide this service, and who's paying the broker?

In most cases, the broker is paid by the lender you've chosen. Depending on which state you're in, your broker may also charge you a fee. However in some states, like South Australia, this is not very common unless the loan is very complex.

Lenders are happy to pay brokers referral fees for connecting them with customers. If the broker hadn't come in contact with you, the lender might have missed out on you as a customer – and anyone who brings paying customers into a business is someone that company wants to look after and keep around.

In essence, think of the broker as the go-between person who helps you save time and energy running around comparing different lenders. A good broker will stay current with new changes in lending criteria from all of the different lenders they work with. Knowing who has the best deal for your mortgage can be a lot more work than you think if you try to do it alone.

How do you find a good broker?

Now that you know what a broker does, how they get paid and why they're definitely worth speaking with, it's time to find a good one. So, how do you do that?

Well, how about I tell you a story of how *not* to find a broker? Unfortunately, it's my story from the first time I bought a property.

I was 21 years old and had no idea what I was doing when I bought my first property. I was working in the outback of South Australia, underground as a diamond driller.

For my age, I was earning pretty reasonable money, and I decided to buy an apartment in Adelaide – in a building I had fantasised about living in for years. This was 2007, pre-smartphone tech days, so when I realised I'd need a broker I thought, 'One of the big firms should do the trick; they must be good if they have so much business.'

I walked into the office of one of the biggest mortgage-broking companies in the country (which will remain nameless). I told the lady at the front desk, 'I'd like to buy a house,' and asked if there was someone I could speak to. I was told to take a seat and someone would be with me in a minute.

A few moments later, a man walked up to me and introduced himself. Let's call him Daryl. Daryl asked me a few questions about my work and what my income was, but nothing about me – what I wanted or why I was buying my first place.

I remember him using all of these terms, like LVR and LMI, and talking about redraw facilities as if I should understand the gibberish coming out of his mouth. I didn't feel very comfortable with him, but I thought it must have just been how this was meant to be; it was my first time applying for a loan and I had nothing to compare it with.

After Daryl had all of the details he needed, I got my pre-approval and went out to shop for my new apartment. I found the apartment very quickly and put in an offer that was well below my pre-approval amount. I thought this would be fine. As the clock started ticking down towards settlement day, there seemed to be problem after problem with the lender. Daryl kept coming back to me and saying, 'The bank needed something else, and there's been another delay at head office,' and, 'The bank won't approve the loan until they have this new statement from your employer; they're always changing their minds.'

It felt like I was being given excuse after excuse, but I had no idea what was normal, so I just trusted him and hoped he was doing the right thing by me. What I didn't understand was that my time to get formal finance approval was slowly being eaten up, and I was about to be in default of my purchase contract. I started getting worried that I was about to lose this apartment that I had dreamed about for years, all because of something that was out of my control. To add to the pressure, I was 1000 km away and 400 m underground, working 12-hour days 14 days straight. Every delay Daryl presented me with was even more challenging to fix in the little time frame I had. Most businesses in Adelaide were not open when I woke up at 4.45 am, and I couldn't call them while I was underground.

Selling agent: the real estate agent who is selling the home.

One night after dinner, I got a call from the selling agent notifying me that his vendor was becoming very concerned and was about to serve notice to cancel my contract. By this point, I'd had enough. As soon as I flew home, I called the mortgage-broking company and asked to speak with the manager. We'll call her Tammy. I explained all of my concerns to Tammy about how things were being delayed, why I was told they were being delayed, and just the overall feeling I had about how it was all going. Tammy was not impressed that this was happening within her company. She told me that her organisation prides itself on providing excellent customer service and that this was not a typical transaction. Tammy assured me that things would be taken care of very promptly, and they were. Within about a day, I had the approval that I needed, and I ended up buying my dream apartment and settling on time.

While everything worked out well in the end, I had no idea how close I was to losing it due to having an incompetent broker on my team.

While there is no exact science to picking the right broker, there are a few simple and easy tips I can give you, along with some signs to look for so you can feel comfortable that you're choosing a good and hardworking broker.

Step 1 - Ask friends and family

Ask anyone you know who has bought a house in the last five years which broker they used. This way, you'll get an unbiased opinion on what the broker was like to deal with from a trusted source.

The simplest way to do this is by putting up a post on social media asking for recommendations. Something like this: 'Hey guys, I'm buying a place and need to find a good broker. Who's the best out there?'

The power of social media is incredible! It's best to take full advantage of it where possible. Posting a quick status to a group of friends and family will save you a lot of time and effort. I still don't know why, but people love helping to solve odd problems and offer advice.

Pretty soon, you should have more comments than a '23 Childhood Celebrities – You'll Never Believe What They Look Like Now' post. Every man and his dog should be recommending people to use and tagging different brokers in the post.

You'll quickly find out that people from all walks of life are keen to help and put forward someone they've used in the past.

Step 2 - Do some research

Now that you have a list of recommended contacts, it's time to call them, right?

Not yet. Now it's time to jump on Google and do a bit of stalking. Type in the broker's name and company and check out their online presence. The company they work for should have an online profile for the broker. This way, you can do what's known in real estate as a 'digital interview' before you decide who to speak with.

Step 3 - Make some calls

You should now have two or three names you're happy with. Give them a call and make a time to meet with them face-to-face. Most brokers will come to you, but there are some that you may need to meet at their office or over Zoom.

Meeting your broker

So now that you have a few meetings lined up, what do you need to do to prepare?

In reality, I could write a list of 50 questions to ask a broker, but I won't – because dealing with your broker should be a lot like dealing with a doctor. You're walking into their world of expertise and putting a massive amount of trust in them. You want to know that you can talk normally with them and have them explain things to you in simple terms to give you a clear understanding of the situation. Most good brokers I've spoken with know the right questions to ask you and how to find the right product (loan) for you.

On the flip side to that, if you sit down with a broker and feel like you're being upsold and having words memorised from a sales script spoken at you, that's a sign you're speaking with someone who either doesn't really understand their job, or is just thinking about themselves and the easiest way to get their commission. Humans are actually amazing lie detectors; sometimes you need to learn to listen to that gut instinct. If you feel that something is off when you're having a meeting with your potential broker, that's generally a sign that they're not the right match for you.

Pre-approval

Almost all the boring stuff is out of the way, but there's one thing left to do before you start looking for your new home: get your pre-approval. This is one of the easiest things to get, but all too often I speak with people who have started shopping for their perfect home before they even know how much they have to spend.

Getting pre-approved for your finance is not just about knowing how much you have to spend; it's also about making sure your offer is as attractive as possible to the vendor when you do find the perfect home.

Pre-approval strengthens your offer

Let me explain with a situation I see all too often.

At the time of writing this chapter, I had recently sold a property in the suburbs of Adelaide. I advertised the home for $339,000 to $369,000, supported by a great campaign that generated loads of interest and led to five offers in writing (I'll talk more about offers in chapter 7). The two offers I managed to negotiate to the highest price were above the top end of the asking price, at $371,000 and $375,000.

Under normal circumstances, you would be right in thinking that $375,000 would be the chosen offer any day. However, the buyers offering $375,000 didn't have their finance sorted at all. They told me that they should be fine as they'd spoken to the bank about six months ago, but they didn't have any form of pre-approval in place. The buyers offering $371,000, on the other hand, had their pre-approval in place and were ready to go.

Upon relaying all of the information to the vendors, they felt that taking the offer with shaky financing was too risky – if the finance fell through, they would potentially need to relist the property and perhaps suffer a financial loss. They instead opted to take a solid $371,000 over a maybe $375,000 because they wanted to minimise the risk of the sale falling over – and because the offer was already over the top end of their dream price.

Vendor: the person (or people) selling the property.

I tell this story because it perfectly illustrates why it's essential to be financially organised when it comes to buying a property. The buyers who offered $375,000 fell in love with the property and were good people, which always makes it harder as the selling agent to tell them they have just lost the home they've been looking for because of something so simple. This situation can be avoided very easily by having your finances organised and ready to go before you even start looking at property. If you do this, you won't receive that heartbreaking phone call from the selling agent saying, 'I'm sorry, you missed out because the vendors went with the offer that had pre-approval in place. Better luck next time.'

Pre-approval tells you what you can afford

Having your pre-approval in place isn't just about showing the vendors that you're a reliable option as a buyer; it also gives you a clearer picture of what you can and can't afford.

Imagine this: you've spoken to a family friend who bought a property a few years ago or you used a very generic borrowing power estimate calculator online which indicated that you could probably only borrow about $400,000.

This is less than you hoped, but you start looking for homes a bit smaller than you'd like, outside of the area you would really love to live in, as this is what you need to do to get into the market. As much as this is an exciting time, the homes you are looking at are not quite what you'd imagined buying. Weeks quickly turn into months and before you know it, you've been looking for six months and you can't find anything that's quite right for you. You know you need to make a few compromises, but the process is now becoming frustrating, and all of the excitement has been sucked clean out of it.

I see this every week as an agent: young couples walking into my open homes looking like death warmed up. When I ask them how long they've been looking, the answer is generally between 6 and 12 months. I can see all the fun of finding their first home has been completely sucked from the situation, and I'm standing in front of two people who are fed up. Unfortunately, the rest of the conversation all too often goes like this:

Me: *So, when you guys do find the right place, are you ready to pounce on it? Is your financing pre-approved, your deposit in place, your conveyancer locked in... you know, all of that stuff?*

Buyers: *Yeah, we're ready.*

Me: *Great. So, you've sat down with a broker and had your pre-approval done?*

Buyers: *Well, no, but we both earn good money, so we know we'll get a loan.*

Me: *Okay, so how did you both come to choose this price bracket to shop in?*

Buyers: *Well, we just figured that's all we could get because we only have a $60,000 deposit and we looked at an online calculator.*

Me: *What if you could get approved for $100,000 more than that – do you think you would have found the right home already?*

Buyers: *Yeah, probably, but we couldn't get that much money.*

Me: *Have you asked a broker?*

Buyers: *Well, no, but we just know we couldn't.*

Me: *With all due respect, how do you know if you haven't asked? It only takes about 20 minutes and could save you another six months of looking. I'm happy to keep seeing you at opens, but I don't think that's a mutual feeling.*

Buyers: *Yeah, I guess we could get our pre-approval done.*

While the above situation is technically hypothetical, unfortunately I see it all too often. It usually ends with me calling the buyers back about three weeks later to find out they have their pre-approval and were pleasantly surprised at how much extra they could borrow, and now have a contract on a house they wouldn't even have looked at six months ago.

It's not just about the time saving, either. Think about this situation for a minute. At the time of writing (2021), if this couple was renting the average house in the cheapest Aussie capital city of Perth according to thepropertynerds.com.au ($390 average weekly rent) to the most expensive of Canberra ($595 average weekly rent) over a six-month period, they would have paid between $10,140 to $15,470 in rent.

That rent money could have gone towards paying off their home loan if they had their pre-approval in place first and not wasted six months looking at all the wrong houses.

If I told you that you could potentially have an extra $10,140 to $15,470 to pay off your new home loan, and all you need to do is go to a 20-minute meeting that won't cost you anything, and this will put you ahead of most other buyers in the market, can you honestly think of any good reason not to do it?

That's what I thought. Good!

Understanding finance speak

Just before we get into looking at your budget and what kind of property you're going to buy, I'll briefly give you a few quick translation tips. The financial world is filled with massive amounts of jargon; it's no different when you're buying a home to live in. One thing that should give you a big confidence boost is understanding two of the common terms used in the property lending world. These terms are:

1. loan-to-value ratio (LVR)

2. lenders mortgage insurance (LMI).

While your broker should explain these terms to you, some may not. I find that when people talk to you about things you're not supposed to understand, in a way that makes you feel that you should understand them, it can make you feel stupid and uncomfortable – when really, the person assuming your knowledge is the one being a numpty. Just in case you are in a situation where someone starts talking in this lingo you'll be confident and calm, understanding exactly what's being said.

Loan-to-value ratio (LVR)

LVR is really just a fancy way of describing how much money the bank needs to put in to complete the purchase in addition to the deposit you're putting down on the property.

Loan-to-value ratio (LVR): the ratio of your loan amount against the value of the property you are purchasing; the loan amount divided by the value of the property.

Let's use a nice round number to make this simple. Say you're buying a home worth $1,000,000. You have a $200,000 deposit, and you need the bank to put in the rest of the money – $800,000. This situation would give you a loan-to-value ratio of 80:20 –more commonly known in the lending world as an 80:20 LVR.

If you only had a deposit of $50,000 in this situation, then you would need the lender to put up $950,000 – which would give you a 95:5 LVR.

Lenders mortgage insurance (LMI)

LMI is an insurance a lender may require you to take out if it feels your LVR is too high. At the time of writing (2021), you typically won't need to pay LMI if you have more than a 20 per cent deposit. If your deposit is under the 20 per cent mark, you will most likely need to pay LMI. Generally, the lower your deposit, the higher your LVR will be – and the more expensive your LMI will be.

The really important thing to remember is that LMI does not protect you as the consumer; this insurance protects the bank if you were to default on the loan.

Lenders mortgage insurance (LMI): an insurance payment that protects the lender if you default on (fail to pay) your home loan.

LMI is generally tacked on to the mortgage and paid off over the life of the loan (rather than it being an upfront cost), however make sure to check this with your broker as individual circumstances may differ.

If you can avoid paying LMI, it's a cost well avoided. However, if it's the difference between getting into the market or renting for another two, three, or four years, then it might be worth considering taking the financial hit.

In a nutshell

- Speaking with a good mortgage broker first not only has the potential to save you a huge stack of cash, it should also get you in the driver's seat with a pre-approval that could put you ahead of your competition when buying your property.

- Make a time with the broker you feel most comfortable with and bring all of the paperwork they tell you to bring; it's time to get you pre-approved!

- Get your head around some of the key terms you'll hear as you move through the finance process.

🎧 Listen

If you would like to learn more about borrowing and how to make yourself more attractive to lenders, listen to episode 73 of the Pizza and Property podcast: 'How Could I Buy 6+ Properties on an Average Wage? – With Fane Levy.'

I totally understand you're probably not interested in buying multiple properties right now, but there is a lot of great information in this episode that will help you make yourself stand out to leaders for all the right reasons – whether you're buying 1 or 100 properties.

Another good episode to listen to is episode 81: 'Seven Things to Know when the Leader Says No'. This episode will walk you through some amazing tricks and tips to put you in the driver's seat and increase your chances of getting the approval you need.

2.

FREE MONEY?

I'm gonna start a band and call it 'Free Beer' so when
people see a sign that reads 'Free Beer tomorrow @ 9:00pm'
everyone will be there.

BENDER, *FUTURAMA*

I still remember talking to people about the First Home Owner
Grant (FHOG) before I'd bought my first property. I had no idea
what it was or how to get it. Back in 2007, when I bought my first
piece of Australia, you didn't need to build the property to be
eligible for the grant like you do now in South Australia. Because
of this I very luckily received a bonus $7000 FHOG to put towards
my new purchase. I can still remember my mum saying to me, 'Oh,
that's wonderful news, Shorty!' (Yes, my mum calls me Shorty.)
'That should pay for all your stamp duty costs and give you a little to
put into your deposit.'

I smiled back incredulously while slowly and politely nodding.
Mum hadn't bought a house since 1981; as much as her excitement
for me was very sweet, I had to explain to her that the $7000 was
great, but it didn't even come close to paying my stamp duty – let
alone this thing called LMI that I'd never heard of, and all the other

costs. Also, there certainly wouldn't be any left over for a deposit. Still excited for me, she smiled and said, 'It's still free money!'

Unless you're one of those lotto winners who strikes it rich only to lose it all and then some, I think it's pretty safe to say that free money is one of the best things ever! I get a little excited when find $20 in some old jeans I haven't worn in ages, so when the government is handing out thousands of dollars to eligible first home buyers, surely you get a bit more excited than you do for your standard cash grab in an old pair of jeans.

You've more than likely heard people talking about the FHOG before, but what exactly is it, and how does it work? That's exactly what we're going to talk about in this chapter.

First Home Owner Grant (FHOG): a national scheme funded by the states and territories that awards a one-off grant to first home buyers who satisfy all the eligibility criteria.

Before I fill you up with too much excitement about free money you may or may not be able to claim, let's answer some of the basic fundamental questions first, to see if you'll even be eligible for the grant.

As you work your way through this chapter, you'll learn the answers to these questions:

- How do I apply for the grant?
- When will the grant be paid if I'm eligible?
- Can the grant be used as my deposit?
- How much is the grant in my state?
- What's the basic eligibility for the grant?
- What's the maximum I can spend?
- Do I need to build or can I buy established?

ⓘ **Note**

After COVID-19 hit in 2020, the federal government introduced a new grant scheme named HomeBuilder. It was rolled out quickly and for several economic reasons that go way beyond the fundamentals of general property buying. The timeline for how long this grant will last has changed a few times; because of this, this grant and several other government incentives will not be covered in the book. While I do encourage you to google and check if this grant or a version of it is available at the time of reading, it is very possible it will no longer be available and something else might be in its place.

How do I apply for the grant?

The application process is slightly different in every state and territory. In order to make the process as simple as possible when applying for the grant, make sure you speak with your mortgage broker about starting the application process once you have decided to commit to purchasing. Make sure your broker is an approved agent or can set you on the right path to send your application through the right channel.

When will the grant be paid?

Each state and territory varies in terms of when payment will be made to eligible applicants. If you're building your first home, the grant is typically paid when the foundations are laid; if you're buying an established home, generally the grant is paid at settlement. Typically the grant is paid to the lender and used in conjunction with the deposit for the loan on the property or build.

Can I use the FHOG as my deposit?

The short answer to this question is no; unless you intend to buy a property that is about $50,000 and meets all the relevant FHOG criteria, chances are you're going to need to use the grant in addition to your deposit, not *as* your deposit. I'm fairly certain this $50,000 house example won't apply to 99 per cent of people reading this book, but just in case it does apply to you, there is one more thing you will need to take into consideration. When a lender is assessing your borrowing eligibility they will usually want to make sure you have something called "genuine savings". This is normally done to make sure you haven't just had a rich uncle deposit $100k into your account for a week that they later take out to make it look like you have a great relationship with money. As general rule of thumb a lender will want to see "genuine savings" for a period of at least three months.

FHOG requirements per state and territory

One of the really important things to remember about the FHOG is that it works slightly differently in each state and territory – not only in terms of how much money you're potentially eligible to receive, but also the kinds of properties that are eligible and the criteria you need to meet.

Due to these differences I'm going to address the FHOG requirements by each state and territory, because as much as I find it interesting to understand how every state works in its own variations, I'm going to take a wild stab in the dark and guess you'd rather skip past all the other states and just get to the information that's potentially going to put some free cash in your pocket. So feel free to skip to the state or territory you're buying in to get the information that's right for you.

In addition to the FHOG, state governments may have other incentive schemes and programs designed to help first home buyers get into the market – such as the New South Wales First Home Buyer Assistance Scheme (FHBAS). I have not included information about these additional schemes in this book, because they can sometimes be introduced and then disappear soon after.

(!) Note

The information in this section is intended as a guide only, and details may change. To confirm the latest information and make sure you're not missing out on any potential grants that are applicable to your state or territory, flip to the references section at the back of the book or visit **pizzaandproperty.com** and click on the 'getting started' tab to find the links to the current government websites.

New South Wales

Being a first home buyer in New South Wales comes with its own challenges; if you're a Sydneysider, even more so. While you live in arguably one of the most vibrant cities in the world, this amazing lifestyle comes at a cost. Sydney is – according to Effie Zahos, editor for Canstar – among the three most unaffordable cities in the world for property. Every last cent you can get towards your property purchase when living in such an expensive but vibrant city is going to make your purchase all the more easy.

Table 2.1: The FHOG in New South Wales

Grant amount:	$10,000
Basic eligibility:	You must be an individual (not a company or trust).
	At least 1 applicant must be an Australian citizen or permanent resident.

Each applicant must be over 18.

Generally must be a genuine first purchase for all applicants.

You must not have received a FHOG previously.

You or one of the other applicants must reside in the property for a minimum of 6 continuous months, commencing within 12 months of the completion of the build or settlement of the purchase; however, you may still be eligible if you purchased a residential property after 1 July 2000 and didn't live in it for more than 6 continuous months.

If you are in the Australian Defence Force you may be exempt from the 6-month rule.

Max price: Newly constructed home: $600,000
Building the home: $750,000

Property type: Newly constructed
Building the home

Northern Territory

The Northern Territory has no maximum limit on the purchase price of your new home. Depending on your budget, this might mean nothing or it might mean amazing things. Something I see all the time as a sales agent is young couples buying or building a beautiful new home knowing full well they want to have two or three little people, a dog, a cat, a boat and all the other things a lot of people want in life. They know this is what they want but they still only build or buy a home for their current lifestyle. Obviously your budget needs to allow this, but if you can build just one extra bedroom or give yourself that little bit more space, it could be the difference between selling every three to five years and paying stamp duty, moving costs, agents fees and the rest of the costs involved in buying and selling, or keeping all of that cash in your pocket and potentially paying down your mortgage quicker – or maybe even having the money to start investing in property.

Either way, the point I'm trying to make isn't about financially stretching yourself to the limit; it's about taking advantage of a grant that has no price limit and building to your budget, but also for the lifestyle you want in the near future.

Table 2.2: The FHOG in the Northern Territory

Grant amount:	$10,000
Basic eligibility:	You must be an individual (not a company or trust).
	At least 1 applicant must be an Australian citizen or permanent resident.
	At least 1 applicant must be over 18.
	You must not have received a FHOG previously.
	Must be a genuine first purchase for all applicants (possible exception for investment properties purchased within particular timeframes – check the relevant website for more details).
	At least 1 applicant must reside in the property for a minimum of 6 continuous months, commencing within 12 months of the completion of the build or settlement of the purchase.
Max price:	No maximum
Property type:	Newly constructed Building the home Substantially renovated home

Queensland

As well as the beautiful beaches, warm weather and Great Barrier Reef, Queensland is one of the states that has some pretty awesome terms in the way the state government looks at people who have started their property journey as 'rent-vestors'. If you have owned an interest in a property since 1 July 2000 that you can prove you have never lived in, you may still be eligible for the grant. In my Pizza and Property podcast I speak with so many first home buyers and new investors all around the country. The fact that in Queensland and some other states you can still be eligible for the grant after you have owned an investment property is something that is relatively unknown. Small pieces of information like this can sometimes be the difference between getting an extra $15,000 in your bank account or leaving it for your premier to spend however he or she sees fit.

Table 2.3: The FHOG in Queensland

Grant amount:	$15,000
Basic eligibility:	You must be an individual (not a company or trust).
	At least 1 applicant must be an Australian citizen or permanent resident.
	Each applicant must be over 18 (possible discretion for age requirement).
	You must not have received a FHOG previously.

Must be a genuine first purchase for all applicants (possible exception for investment properties purchased within particular timeframes – check the relevant website for more details).

At least 1 applicant must reside in the property for a minimum of 6 continuous months, commencing within 12 months of the completion of the build or settlement of the purchase.

Max price:	$750,000
Property type:	Newly constructed Building the home Substantially renovated home

South Australia

In South Australia the FHOG is not as flexible as in some other states. In overly simplified terms, you need to build or purchase a new home and have never owned a home before to qualify. There are not the same kinds of exceptions or special differences you might find in other states, which is both a good and bad thing depending on how you look at it. If you live in South Australia and are reading this section of the chapter thinking, 'I've never even thought about building a home,' I do strongly recommend you talk with a few builders first to get a better understanding of whether it's a process you feel comfortable with. If you're planning on building anyway, then great! But changing such a big commitment like this is not something I'd ever suggest just to get a grant, no matter how tempting free money is.

Table 2.4: The FHOG in South Australia

Grant amount:	$15,000
Basic eligibility:	You must be an individual (not a company or trust).
	At least 1 applicant must be an Australian citizen or permanent resident.
	Each applicant must be over 18.
	Must be a genuine first purchase for all applicants.
	You must not have received a FHOG previously.
	All applicants must reside in the property for a minimum of 6 continuous months, commencing within 12 months of the completion of the build or settlement of the purchase.
Max price:	$575,000
Property type:	Newly constructed Building the home

Tasmania

Tasmania has to be one of the most generous when it comes to the FHOG. Not only is Tasmanian real estate already lighter on the hip pocket than a lot of its east coast mainland counterparts, it also gives the largest grant out of any state to first home buyers – which is a double awesome in my opinion! Pay less and get more is only ever a good thing.

One of the other great things about Tasmania's FHOG is that there's no maximum spend to qualify for the grant. So if you have already nailed saving your deposit and have a massive stack of cash, go you – that's amazing! You might be able to take advantage of this grant in a way that you only can in Tassie and the Northern Territory by keeping your eligibility while building a property to whatever budget you and your lender agree on.

Table 2.5: The FHOG in Tasmania

Grant amount:	$20,000
Basic eligibility:	You must be an individual (not a company or trust).
	At least 1 applicant must be an Australian citizen or permanent resident.
	Each applicant must be over 18.
	You must not have received a FHOG previously.
	Must be a genuine first purchase for all applicants (possible exception for investment properties purchased within particular timeframes – check the relevant website for more details).
	All applicants must reside in the property for a minimum of 6 continuous months, commencing within 12 months of the completion of the build or settlement of the purchase.
Max price:	No maximum
Property type:	Newly constructed Building the home

Victoria

The rivalry between Sydney and Melbourne has been going for over a century. One thing I'm sure Victoria's glad to let New South Wales have is the highest median house price. Friendly rivalries aside, even though Melbourne might not have the highest median house price in the country it's still not what I'd call a cheap place to live.

Table 2.6: The FHOG in Victoria

Grant amount:	$10,000 (metropolitan areas)
	$20,000 (regional areas)*
Basic eligibility:	At least 1 applicant must be an Australian citizen or permanent resident.
	At least 1 applicant must be over 18 (possible discretion for age requirement).
	Must be a genuine first purchase for all applicants (possible exception for investment properties purchased within particular timeframes – check the relevant website for more details).
	You must not have received a FHOG previously.
	At least 1 applicant must reside in the property for a minimum of 12 continuous months, commencing within 12 months of the completion of the build or settlement of the purchase.

Max price:	$750,000
Property type:	Newly constructed
	Building the home
	Substantially renovated home

*Please check if the $20,000 regional FHOG is still available at the time of reading.

Western Australia

Western Australia brings something a little different to the table when it comes to the FHOG, as it is one of the few states or territories that will actually consider a person under the age of 18 to be eligible for the grant. So, on the off chance you're a 16 or 17-year-old reading this book, first of all, hats off to you! You're a superstar! But also, this is a good sign not to give up on your dream of owning a property at an amazingly young age.

Western Australia also gives some flexibility to past ownership between the dates of 1 July 2000 and 1 July 2004. When fact-checking this section of the chapter, I must admit this section in particular was a bit hard to wrap my head around because of the way it is worded: in typically confusing government legal speak. Confusion or not, if you have owned a property in the past and are wanting to purchase now and apply for the FHOG, make sure you go through the details with your lender to see if your specific situation applies to the criteria.

Lastly, Western Australia has a unique way of breaking up the maximum purchase price of the FHOG by using the line of the 26th parallel. For all of you that were exactly like me a while back and have no idea what the 26th parallel is, it's a circle of latitude that sits 26 degrees from the equator – how cool is that for a random pub trivia fact you can impress your friends with? This line is used to divide the FHOG maximum spend between $750,000 south of the 26th parallel and $1,000,000 north of the 26th parallel.

Table 2.7: The FHOG in Western Australia

Grant amount:	$10,000
Basic eligibility:	At least 1 applicant must be an Australian citizen or permanent resident.
	Each applicant must be over 18 (possible discretion for age requirement).
	You must not have received a FHOG previously.
	Must be a genuine first purchase for all applicants (possible exception for investment properties purchased within particular timeframes – check the relevant website for more details).
	All applicants must reside in the property for a minimum 6 continuous months, commencing within 12 months of the completion of the build or settlement of the purchase.
Max price:	$750,000 (south of the 26th parallel) $1,000,000 (north of the 26th parallel)
Property type:	Newly constructed Building the home Substantially renovated home

Australian Capital Territory

Fun fact about the *Back to the Future* movies: *Back to the Future Part II* is the only movie sequel in history to revisit the first movie during the sequel's storyline! You're probably thinking, 'Todd, that's a fun fact and all but I'm here to learn about the FHOG in the Australian Capital Territory.' Right you are! However, if you want to be eligible for the FHOG in the territory, you'll need to jump in your time machine and start building your home on or before 1 July 2019.

It's not all bad news, though. For starters, you just learnt a pretty cool fact about one of the best movie franchises of all time. Also, the territory government has issued a different scheme called the Home Buyer Concession Scheme; if you meet the eligibility criteria, your stamp duty could be waived.

Just in case you're thinking that's not a very good deal, depending on how much you're wanting to spend on your first purchase it's possibly going to be a bigger saving overall for you than being given $10,000 like most of the other states and territories.

If you were to spend $500,000 it should be an approximate saving of over $11,000, but if you're shopping at Canberra's current median house price of $850,000 you would be saving a whopping $28,000! Now that's a great discount to get when you're buying your first home.

Am I eligible if this is not my first property purchase?

In most states, you may still be eligible for the FHOG if you have owned a property in the past that you have never lived in as your principal place of residence (PPR). In South Australia it doesn't matter if you owned an investment property or if you lived in the property as your home – if you bought a property previously, that's it! You can never be eligible for the FHOG. In other states, however, it's a little different. You may still be eligible for the FHOG if you or your partner purchased property that you have not lived in as your home. For example, say you purchased your first property and have rented it out ever since. Since you have never lived there yourself, this house is not considered to be your first residential home and you may still be eligible for the FHOG. Checking a simple detail like this in the state you're buying in could be the difference between having a big chunk of free money or maybe missing out because you assumed you wouldn't be eligible.

Principal place of residence (PPR): the property in which you reside, occupy and live as your home.

What does 'substantially renovated' mean?

In some states, buying a 'substantially renovated' home could make you eligible for the FHOG.

But what *is* a substantially renovated home? That's a good question and I'm glad you asked.

The details differ state by state, but might include factors such as:

- most of the home being removed or replaced as part of the renovation
- the home not being lived in or sold since being renovated.

While it is very exciting that buying a substantially renovated home could potentially make you eligible for the grant, personally I'm not a big fan of the word 'most' in the first bullet point above. Anything that is so open to interpretation means you would absolutely want to make sure the property you intend to purchase qualifies for the grant before committing to buying it – especially if you're counting on the grant money to settle on the property. At least, you would want to obtain very clear advice from the governing body in your state or territory.

I know this might sound a bit pedantic, but if my girlfriend says she just wants a teeny-tiny bit of my chocolate bar, as far as I'm concerned most of my chocolate is about to disappear – even as she maintains, 'Todd, you're exaggerating, I hardly touched it.' While I'm obviously making fun of the situation, I truly do want to emphasise the seriousness of making sure you get your checks done on this if you are planning on buying a 'substantially renovated' property –what is 'a little bit' to some could be 'most' to others.

What if I'm not eligible?

If you have figured out you're not going to be able to receive a FHOG, please make sure you treat yourself to a big slice of pizza and a beer – or whatever it is that you do for fun. I know you can't get the grant and that sucks, but the fact that you even took the time to read through this chapter and check means you're more committed to making your property dreams happen than so many people out there. Even though this grant may not happen for you, I can tell you that you're the kind of person that will do better than most when buying property because you're prepared to do the research and do what it takes to make it happen.

If you've just read this chapter and realised you can now get $10,000, $15,000 or maybe $20,000 you didn't even know about, then how cool is that! This should be a day that will forever rival those moments of finding $20 in an old pair of jeans. Congratulations, you're one step closer towards being a homeowner.

In a nutshell

- Check the state and territory government websites that are relevant to where you intend to purchase, and use these as your sources of truth. I've listed the sites for you at the back of the book and on my website at **pizzaandproperty.com**.

- You never know when the governments might increase, decrease or change the criteria of the FHOG.

- Check to see if there are any other government grants, discounts or schemes that you could possibly get some free money from.

- Don't discount the FHOG if you have previously owned an investment property; in some states, you may still be eligible.

3.

SETTING YOUR BUDGET

Budgeting isn't about limiting yourself,
it's about making the things that excite you possible.

– UNKNOWN

I grew up with reasonably good money management skills, having the benefit of being raised by an extremely budget-conscious mother. Dividing up my weekly income into different expense accounts is something I have always done, and I always assumed everyone else did the same.

It wasn't until my late teens that I realised none of my friends did this at all. To them, it was entirely reasonable for a lump sum of money to be paid into their bank account at the start of the week, then disappear in the first couple of days – only for the same thing to happen the following week.

As I grew older, I came to realise that this is how most people manage – or, rather, mismanage – their money.

The more I thought about it, I realised this behaviour was more than just a case of young people being carefree with their fast food job paycheques; it was the beginning of a costly habit that would almost certainly carry over into adulthood.

If you already have your deposit saved up and are on top of your money, that's awesome! I would high-five you right now if I could – because you're a great saver and money manager, which is an excellent skill to have.

But if you look at your bank account regularly and think, 'How am I going to pay for that bill?' or 'Where is all my money going? I just got paid three days ago,' this chapter is probably going to be the most important in the whole book.

If you don't have enough money for an upfront deposit and proof of your ongoing ability to service a mortgage, the banks simply will not lend you the money you need for your new home.

ⓘ Note

Full disclosure: *I am not a financial adviser*. The budgeting tips I'm about to show you are just what I grew up with and thought everyone else did, too. My mother was not a financial whiz, but she was very clever at being able to make the little money she had go a long way. By having an understanding of precisely what was coming in and where it was going, she gave my sister and I things we should have never had growing up as a lower-income family. By all means, speak with a qualified financial adviser. You don't have to take my word for this – I just want to share what works for me.

Planning your budget

For this part of the book, you're going to want to grab a pencil and eraser to fill out the spreadsheet opposite (table 3.1), otherwise grab your laptop or tablet and head to **pizzaandproperty.com** and go to the 'getting started' tab, where you can find a blank copy of the spreadsheet to download. Fill in your income and your outgoings. Not every income or expense item on the spreadsheet will apply to you. For this spreadsheet to be useful, you simply need to fill in the expenses and income that do apply, and ignore those that don't.

Table 3.1: Budget spreadsheet*

Income			
Paycheque 1	$	Child support	$
Paycheque 2	$	Other income	$
Dividend or rental	$	**Income total**	$
Expenses			
House		**Cars and transport**	
Rent/mortgage	$	Loan repayments	$
Utilities, power, water etc.	$	Fuel	$
Internet and phone	$	Registration and insurance	$
Insurance	$	Maintenance	$
Food	$	Public transport or parking	$
Other	$	Other	$
Subtotal	$	**Subtotal**	$
Personal		**Kids**	
Clothing	$	School fees	$
Student loans	$	Clothes	$
Gym and health	$	Sports/activities	$
Health insurance	$	**Subtotal**	$
Date night	$	**Other expenses**	
General spending	$	Gifts	$
Netflix	$	Travel	$
Other	$	Other	$
Subtotal	$	**Subtotal**	$
Totals			
Total outgoings			$
Total income			$
Income minus outgoings = savings total			$

*The information in this book, as well as the tables and charts provided, is for general information only and should not be taken as constituting professional advice from the author. We recommend you seek advice specific to your situation and circumstances from a qualified financial professional.

Have a smartphone or laptop nearby so you can easily log into your internet banking and pull up some of your online bills to fill in the expense section. Some expenses you may not have accurate records for; in these cases, just try to be as honest as you can. If you have a love of new shoes and buy a new pair of Jimmy Choos every week, don't try to hide it. Be honest, and look at what you currently spend. Being completely honest with yourself around a subject like budgeting is absolutely crucial if you're going to actually get what you want. Otherwise, you're just wasting your time filling in a whole page of make-believe numbers that won't get you any closer to buying your new home.

The best way to divide up your expenses is in the same time frame as you're paid – so if you are paid monthly, divide your yearly insurance bill by 12; but if you are paid fortnightly, divide it by 26.

Now, if you're unhappy with what you see, and have found out that not only are you not saving as much as you'd hoped, but you're actually going backwards, *don't* feel bad. This is an excellent opportunity to turn things around and get yourself back on track. Simply erase some of the expenses you think are a bit too high – or maybe you could do without – and relocate the money into your savings section.

Now that you have your budget in place and know how much you need to allow for living expenses, it's time to find a loan amount that suits your lifestyle.

How much can you afford to borrow?

The more money you borrow from a lender, the more money they can make from you – so, in reality, it's in their best interests to lend you the maximum amount possible. But it's not necessarily in *your* best interests to take 100 per cent of what the bank will lend you. For a reality check, take a look at the payments you'll need to make to repay the loan.

Table 3.2 shows the fortnightly repayments on loan amounts ranging from $150,000 to $4 million. I have very deliberately made the difference in loan amounts substantial; this is because of the significant variation in house prices around the country. Just like the rest of the book, I want this section to be helpful whether you live in an outback town buying a $150,000 house, or are about to buy an incredible apartment overlooking the Sydney Harbour Bridge for $4,000,000. What might be expensive to you could be entirely reasonable for someone else, and vice versa.

Table 3.2: Repayment amounts*

Loan amount	Loan duration	Historical interest rate average	Fortnightly repayments	Current interest rate average	Fortnightly repayments
$150,000	30 years	6.0%	$414.87	2.4%	$269.87
$200,000	30 years	6.0%	$553.17	2.4%	$359.82
$250,000	30 years	6.0%	$691.46	2.4%	$449.78
$300,000	30 years	6.0%	$829.75	2.4%	$539.74
$350,000	30 years	6.0%	$968.04	2.4%	$629.69
$400,000	30 years	6.0%	$1106.33	2.4%	$719.65
$450,000	30 years	6.0%	$1244.62	2.4%	$809.60
$500,000	30 years	6.0%	$1382.92	2.4%	$899.56
$600,000	30 years	6.0%	$1659.50	2.4%	$1079.47
$800,000	30 years	6.0%	$2212.68	2.4%	$1439.30
$1,000,000	30 years	6.0%	$2765.85	2.4%	$1799.12
$1,500,000	30 years	6.0%	$4149.00	2.4%	$2698.68
$2,000,000	30 years	6.0%	$5531.69	2.4%	$3598.24
$4,000,000	30 years	6.0%	$11,063.39	2.4%	$7196.48

* The information in this book, as well as the tables and charts provided, is for general information only and should not be taken as constituting professional advice from the author. We recommend you seek advice specific to your situation and circumstances from a qualified financial professional.

At the time of writing this book, the average variable interest rate is around 2.4 per cent, which is an all-time low. Just in case you're reading this book in your early 20s and haven't seen what interest rates have done in the past, I really can't emphasise *all-time low* enough. If you bought a house in 1989, you would have seen interest rates move from 17 per cent to 10 per cent in 1992, then drop even lower to about 6.5 per cent by 1997, only to jump back up to 8 per cent in 2001, bounce around a few percentage points for nearly a decade, then drop to the historical lows we see today of about 2.4 per cent.

Table 3.2 gives both the historical average interest rate of 6 per cent and the current average interest rate of 2.4 per cent. This illustrates what your fortnightly repayments for the same loan amount would be at both interest rates.

Unless you intend to pay off your mortgage in a few years, I believe it's much safer to budget using an interest rate that is closer to the historical standard (6 per cent).

Last time Australian homeowners saw interest rates even close to what we have now, we were still nine years away from landing on the moon, Sydney's median house price was $27,000, and my nana was only in her 20s!

I don't tell you this to try to scare you or put you off buying property. The reason I'm pointing these interest rate changes out is that we all know it's easy to make hay while the sun shines. I believe you need to have a plan for when things aren't as rosy as they are now – or you could find yourself being forced to sell your home you've worked so hard to buy. As Ned Stark says, 'Winter is coming.' As much as I love selling homes for people, I hate watching them go through the unnecessary pain of having to sell because they can't afford their repayments anymore. I have had to help too many people through this situation, so let's make sure you never even get close to it.

Calculating how much you can afford

The best way to decide on a comfortable loan amount is to take your current rental or mortgage expenses and your current fortnightly savings towards your new home deposit, and add the two together to give you what I'll call your comfortable mortgage repayment amount.

Example

Here's an example of calculating a comfortable mortgage repayment amount:

Current rent	= $900 per fortnight
+ Savings	= $500 per fortnight
Comfortable mortgage repayment amount	= $1400 per fortnight
Comfortable mortgage amount	= $500,000 (see table 3.2)

Now, fill out your own figures below:

Current rent	= $_____ per fortnight
+ Savings	= $_____ per fortnight
Comfortable mortgage repayment amount	= $_____ per fortnight
Comfortable mortgage amount	= $_____

How much do I need all up in savings?

Now that you have a much clearer understanding of what a comfortable repayment should look like for you, it's time to think about how much money you will need to save for your deposit and closing costs.

The exact amount you'll need will differ greatly based on:

- what state you're buying in
- whether LMI will apply to your loan
- whether there are there any immediate renovation expenses you'll need to cover
- whether you need to budget for a building and/or pest inspection.

Due to the amount of variations that will come into this, I recommend you take the figures you have worked out in this chapter and run through them with a trusted financial professional. This way you'll have someone in your corner who knows how to work through the specifics of your situation.

In a nutshell

- Have a clear understanding of what you can afford without changing your lifestyle too much before you start shopping for your dream home.

- Work out your outgoings and income and match these with a mortgage amount that fits your specific lifestyle. This will prevent you from being forced to eat vegemite on toast every night of the week for the next 10 years.

- You may need advice from a trusted financial professional to work out how large a deposit you need to save.

PART II

FINDING THE ONE

4.

CHOOSING THE RIGHT HOME

A good life is not lived by chance but by choice.

– KOBI YAMADA

I truly believe we live in one of the most abundant countries in the world. With such a dominant middle class, there are far fewer people living in poverty compared to many other places in the world. In Australia, we have practically free access to education and healthcare, and plenty of government assistance to help people get back on their feet if things get bad. I know we don't have a perfect system, and there is always room for improvement; however, we really do live in the lucky country.

It wasn't until I was driving through the suburbs of St Petersburg, Russia, that I realised this. Russia is a vast, beautiful country with a rich culture and history. If you ever get the chance to go there, I highly recommend you take it. The city of St Petersburg boasts some of the world's most stunning architecture, not to mention fantastic vodka. Driving through the suburbs of St Petersburg completely opened up my eyes to how so many people actually live in Eastern Europe. It's one thing to see it in a documentary on Netflix; it's another to be standing out the front of a real family's home in minus-6-degree weather, seeing living conditions that are below the poverty line, knowing that millions of people in this country are forced to accept this as normal.

I couldn't believe the feeling of appreciation I immediately felt when I witnessed this part of the world firsthand. I saw people throwing buckets of (what I hope was) water out of the windows from these depressing, grey buildings that looked as if they would have been condemned if they were in Australia. Gazing at a sea of colourless, sad accommodation mixed together with mud and old, dirty snow made me realise why Russians stereotypically drink so much vodka. I would, too, if I lived in that part of the country.

I turned to the cab driver and asked in my best attempt at speaking Russian, 'Are we in a bad part of town?'

He looked at me and said in Russian, 'This is Russia.' I slowly turned, looking back out of the window of the cab, just soaking it all in. I really was feeling somewhat overwhelmed by how unaffected everyone was by what I could only think were devastating living conditions.

I would imagine if you never knew any different, and didn't have any other options, you would have to accept this as just how you and your family would live.

As Australians, most of us do have options, and plenty of them; possibly too many! This is precisely what this chapter is about: how to pick the right home from a massive sea of options.

'How are we going to do that?' I hear you ask. By using two different buying methods that can help you narrow down the object of your search:

1. Wants, needs and won'ts

2. Beautiful, close and cheap.

Following these methods will help you steer away from problem properties and towards the right home for you and your needs.

Wants, needs and won'ts

One of the most common mistakes I see people make when it comes to buying their first property, or even their second, is thinking about the things that they would *like* to have instead of what they actually *need* from a home.

Don't get me wrong: your home should be somewhere you feel happy to come back to. It should be somewhere you look forward to spending time with your friends and family: having a BBQ, reading on the balcony or rugging up on the couch to binge-watch your most recent Netflix addiction.

While it is so important to live in a home you're happy with and feel comfortable in, it's essential for your new home to complement your lifestyle – that is, all of the needs in your life. I'm sure, if given a chance, we would all be living somewhere incredible – maybe a penthouse in the city, a beachfront mansion on the coast or perhaps a beautiful manor house far out in the country. If you're about to buy an incredible home that could be featured on the cover of a magazine, that's awesome! But unfortunately, not all of us have this option to buy the amazing cover-photo home.

In my experience, the majority of us rarely seem to act on the simple solution. As people, we can have this thought process that says something along the lines of, 'If it's that easy, why isn't everyone else doing it?' This chapter will help you balance the two lists: what you want in a property alongside what you need to live the life you really want. One of the best ways to do this is by introducing a third list, which is usually very easy to write: it's a won'ts list. Listing all these things you won't put up with in a new property is a great way to quickly exclude properties that are not right for you.

At the time of writing this chapter, my partner and I are looking to buy another property; not as in investment, this time – it will be our first family home together. She grew up in a small town, so a beautiful, quiet location is extremely important to her – as well as being close to excellent schools for our future children. So for her, the two big things on the won't list are main roads, and areas that are more than 10 minutes from a quality school. My won'ts are living on a small block of land (less than 300 m²) and being more than 20 minutes from the CBD.

Knowing our respective won'ts is great because it drastically helps to refine our search, eliminating a lot of wasted time looking at properties that just won't be right for us. For example, if a property pops up that is in a quiet cul-de-sac five minutes walk from the best school, but it's built on a small courtyard block, my partner knows not to bother with it.

By understanding what you *want*, what you *need* and what you *won't* put up with, you significantly increase your chances of finding the right home within your budget – and you'll do it so much quicker than if you're blindly looking around for months on end.

Compiling your wants, needs and won'ts lists

I really urge you to make a commitment to yourself right now to compile a lists of your wants, needs and won'ts. Stop reading or listening to this book right now and call your significant other (if you're buying with someone else), or just book a time with yourself to get this done.

It's easy; just open a bottle of wine or beer, or pour a coffee – whatever it is that you like to do when you're unwinding – and start thinking about what you'd like in a home. Let your mind wander a little if you like. Maybe you've always wanted a big 10 by 10 m shed to house the classic car you're fixing up; perhaps you're dreaming of a balcony with a city view. As long as it's nothing too crazy, this list will be beneficial.

Once you've finished with your list of all the things you want in a home, it's time to move on to your needs. The most important thing when putting your needs down on paper is honesty. Really try your best not to write anything on the need list that is actually a want.

For example, I know I really (really!) want a bookcase that's actually a door into a secret room, just like Batman. It would be so cool! And, mark my words, I will have a bookcase door one day. However, if I tried to convince my partner a secret Batman door should be on our need list, what do you think she's more likely to say? 'Oh wow, Todd, you're absolutely right! We need that. You know what? How have we lived all this time without a secret bat cave? That's definitely on the need list.' Or:

'Todd, I love you, and I know you love Batman, but that's clearly not something we need. Do you think maybe we could put that on the want list? Maybe somewhere towards the end of it.'

The seven-year-old in me really wishes she'd give me the first response, but the rational adult knows without a doubt her reaction will be a lot closer to the second version – and rightfully so.

This exercise will only help you if you are *completely* honest with what you write down. If you do get to the point of feeling stuck between a want and a need, try to think of it this way:

- A *want* is something that will generally raise your standard of living.

- A *need* is something that will usually keep your standard of living consistent.

- A *won't* is something that will generally lower your standard of living.

Now, let's go through some questions to get your mind moving in the right direction. There are many more wants, needs and wont's to consider, but these should help you get the ball rolling if you're having trouble getting started.

(!) **Note**

Visit my website **pizzaandproperty.com** to download a handy template that will help you compile your lists.

Wants

Here are some common wants to get you started:

- Have you always wanted to live in a house with a pool?

- Would you love to live near the beach?

- Do you love the idea of having a new, large kitchen with all the bells and whistles?

- Would you love to have a room with a view?

- Would you like to live in the city?

- Would you like to buy a character home?

- Have you always wanted to live on acreage?

- Would you like a brand-new bathroom with a spa bath and floor-to-ceiling tiles?

- Have you always wanted a home theatre?

- Do you want a triple-car garage?

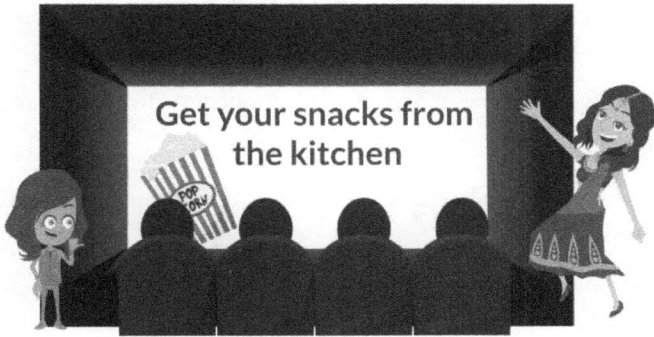

Get your snacks from the kitchen

I'd be surprised if you didn't answer 'yes' to at least seven of those questions. Who wouldn't want a new massive kitchen with a view overlooking a pool in a character home? That sounds amazing! Just to be clear, I'm not saying this to get you to start thinking about real estate porn, I'm just trying to get your brain rolling for the task at hand.

Next is the more conservative stuff: your needs.

Needs

In contrast to your wants list, the purpose of your needs list is to make sure you don't end up living in a home that isn't right for you. Here are some questions to get you started:

- Do you work on call and need to be no more than 10 minutes from work?

- Do you run a business from home and need to have storage for tools or stock?

- Do you often eat out with friends and spend a lot of money on cabs?

- Are your children turning into teenagers who need their own bathroom?

- Do you have a weekly or daily social commitment that you need to be close to?

- Do you need to be in a particular school zone for the kids?

- Do you need space for a home office?

- Do you need the home to be single storey because stairs are an issue?

- Do you have family members who will be coming to live with you soon, who will need a separate living space?

- Do you and your partner both need undercover and secure car spaces?

Won'ts

For your own benefit, make sure you're only putting real won'ts on this next list. If you fill the list with a long line of things that you would actually be okay with, you'll just be making your buying experience even harder than it needs to be. Here are a few standard won'ts I hear from buyers regularly:

- I won't live more than 10 km away from work.

- I won't live next to a shopping centre.

- I won't live closer than 10 km to my in-laws.

- I won't live in a house with a pool.
- I won't live in a house with only one bathroom.
- I won't live in a house with a big backyard.
- I won't live in a large apartment building.

Now your mind should be on the right track. Pull out a pen and start writing down your list of wants, needs and won'ts using table 4.1 on the next page.

Table 4.1: My wants, needs and won'ts

Wants	Needs	Won'ts
1	1	1
2	2	2
3	3	3
4	4	4
5	5	5
6	6	6
7	7	7
8	8	8
9	9	9
10	10	10
11	11	11
12	12	12
13	13	13
14	14	14
15	15	15
16	16	16
17	17	17
18	18	18
19	19	19
20	20	20

If you need several copies of your wants, needs and won'ts list, simply visit my website **pizzaandproperty.com** and print off any of the templates or tools found in the book.

If you're reading this sentence, it should only be because you've finished your wants, needs and won'ts lists. If you haven't finished them yet, please, for your own sake, stop reading now and go back to the lists and finish them. If you don't, the rest of this chapter won't be very helpful.

Starting your search

Now that you have your wants, needs, and won'ts listed, it's time to put them into action. The benefit of putting these simple lists together is they make sure your new home gives you everything you need, as much of what you want as possible and absolutely none of your won'ts.

To begin with, take a look at your needs list and pick out any need that is geographical. It could be that you need to be no more than a 2 km walk to your kids' school, or perhaps a maximum distance of 20 km to drive to work . Or maybe you can't be any further than 5 km from your parents because they need looking after regularly. It really doesn't matter what it is, just make sure you circle it – or all of them, if there are multiple geographical needs.

On the off chance you don't have any geographical needs at all, well, the world's your oyster. You can buy property wherever you want. I really mean this. Have a long and honest think about the possibilities for your own sake. Most of the time, when someone buys a property, they need to be close to at least one thing – whether it's for study, family or work. But if you live a 'laptop lifestyle' or have just received an inheritance giving you the freedom to live wherever you want, start googling – and make sure you send me a selfie in front of your new place, in whatever exotic location you end up choosing.

Looking at your geographical needs first is a great way to very quickly narrow down the suburbs/areas for your property search.

Next, remember your maximum borrowing amount you calculated in chapter 3? Write that figure down, then grab your smartphone and open up the Domain real estate app.

It really doesn't matter if you use Domain or realestate.com.au – I think they both have their strengths and weaknesses in different areas. The only reason I suggest using the Domain app for this exercise is because (at the time of writing) Domain has created a handy searching function to help you find your right home, in the place you want it. So just for now, make sure you've downloaded the Domain app, and you're ready to search.

Make sure you have your wants and needs list close by as well, and simply follow the steps below:

- Open up Domain on your phone.
- Tap on the 'filters' tab to start entering in your wants, needs and won'ts details.
- Leave the area and surrounding suburbs blank for now.
- Enter in your maximum budget plus an extra approximately 10 per cent (only in case your perfect home is currently overpriced).
- If your property type is a need, select the correct option; if it's not a need, then leave it blank.
- Adjust the bedrooms, bathrooms, car spaces and land size only if they're on your needs list. Otherwise, leave them alone at this stage as well.
- If you have a need that is a little different from the general search criteria, enter it into the 'keyword' or 'other information' section.
- Leave 'exclude under offer' switched off; you're better off seeing a property that could come back on the market than not seeing it.
- And lastly, tap 'search'.

Now comes the enjoyable part! Here's how to use my favourite feature of the Domain app:

- Click the map view and, by pinching your fingers together on the screen, slowly zoom out until you can see the location you've listed as a geographical need.

- Now zoom out until you can see the approximate maximum distance you can be away from those geographical needs.

- Next, gently tap the icon that looks like a hand with some string around the finger.

- Using your finger, draw a circle around the radius of your geographical area. Even if at first this includes a few areas that you're not really excited about, I'm going to urge you just to have faith in what I'm recommending: you're better off swiping past a property you don't want than missing one that would have been perfect if you only saw it.

- Lastly, tap the 'list view' tab.

What you should now have in front of you is a complete list of all the properties on the market that should match your needs and budget. Simply start searching through all of the properties and use the rest of the items on your wants, needs and won'ts lists to narrow your search. To make it even easier for you to keep track of the properties you like, make sure to tap the little star up in the top right-hand corner of the screen and save the property to your shortlist.

'But wait for a second, Todd... none of these properties look like the right home for me or look like what I want. What do I do now?'

If you find that your search only provides you with properties that fall a little short of what you'd like, you need to refine your list further using my beautiful, close and cheap method.

Beautiful, close and cheap

You know how some things just stick with you from your younger years, but you can't explain why? I was a massive fan of *The Simpsons* growing up, and I'm still confident I can remember just about any quote from the show in an instant. But if you ask me what I had for lunch yesterday, I'd need to think for a minute – and I probably still couldn't tell you what I had with 100 per cent confidence.

Something a little more useful than my ability to remember *The Simpsons* quotes is a comment one of my friends made over a few drinks one evening. He was a pretty successful businessman at the time, and is now one of the best in his field. I needed his advice on improving my very first business venture when I was 19.

A few drinks in, sitting in a bar on Rundle Street, Adelaide, I began to shift the conversation to business. I asked him his advice on how I could keep costs down without compromising on the quality of my overall project.

I remember him looking at me sternly, holding a Jack Daniels and Diet Coke in one hand and shaking his other hand at me like a teacher, saying, 'Todd, there are three things you want in business: you want it to be *good,* you want it to be *fast* and you want it to be *cheap.* The thing that most people don't figure out is that you'll only ever get two of them. If it's good and it's fast, it's not going to be cheap. If it's cheap and it's fast, it's not going to be very good. And if it's cheap and it's good, it's not going to be very fast.'

I have always remembered that little saying and when I began to sell real estate, I realised it applied to buying houses as much as it did building businesses. There are three things everyone wants in a property (see figure 5.1):

1. They want it to be *beautiful.*
2. They want it to be as *close* to what they want or need as possible.
3. They want it as *cheap* as possible.

Figure 5.1: Beautiful, close and cheap

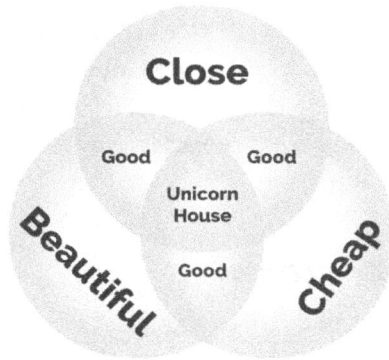

Remember, you'll only ever get two of these three factors. It's up to you to decide which you are most willing to compromise on.

Beautiful

Unless you're buying a property that you intend to renovate, you want it to be as beautiful as possible. This might mean you're looking for an entirely renovated house, or something completely different (because beauty is in the eye of the beholder). Generally speaking, though, the beauty factor implies size and style. I've never seen a 100 m² falling-apart beach shack make the cover of a home magazine.

Close

Getting a property that is as close to meeting your wants and needs as possible is a massive bonus. And, geographically speaking, being five minutes from the city for work or a short walk to the beach for a lazy weekend is fantastic. As I'm reasonably confident you're already aware, this kind of convenience comes at a price.

Cheap

'Cheap' is a somewhat relative term. What's cheap to me might be incredibly expensive to you, or vice versa. When I use the word 'cheap', I don't mean this in any kind of an insulting way, like being a cheapskate. I use the term 'cheap' to refer to your budget, and how much beauty and close proximity you're trying to purchase relative to it.

When you're not having any luck

If you have followed all the steps above and feel that you're still not getting closer to your first or new home, then one of the three factors (beautiful, close or cheap) has got to give a little – or maybe even a lot. It may be that something on your lists of needs and wants, or the budget, must be adjusted slightly.

I know this isn't fun. As a matter a fact, it's the exact opposite of fun. But if you really don't have any suitable properties coming up in your search results after completing the previous steps, something must change to get you into your new home.

First things first: revisit your budget breakdown from the previous chapter. Have a more detailed look through and see if it's reasonable to find an extra $50, $100 or maybe even $200 a fortnight in extra cash. You might be able to achieve this by cutting back on something you enjoy doing, even if it's only for a few years; or you may be able to pick up a few more hours at work to increase your income, bringing you up to the borrowing level that matches your wants and needs.

A $500,000 loan at 2.4% interest has fortnightly repayments of $899.

A $550,000 loan at 2.4% interest has fortnightly repayments of $990.

That's a difference of $45.50 per week.

If you can't compromise on any of your needs at all, maybe it's time to compromise on some of your spending habits. If $45.50 per week is holding you back from your perfect home, it might be worth cutting back on a few other things you don't need. If you take a small percentage from several areas, you might not even really notice a difference.

For example:

- If you're spending $220 per week on your grocery shop, is there any way you could cut that back just a bit to $200 per week? *That's $20 savings per week.*

- Do you buy a takeaway coffee every weekday? Maybe you could cut that back to just once a week. *That's around $15 savings per week.*

- Are you spending $60 a month on a gym membership that you rarely use? Cancel it and run around the neighbourhood for free. *That's almost $15 savings per week.*

Just these three ideas alone would give you a saving of approximately $50 per week which is more than you need and potentially brings you closer to affording the property you really want.

I would like to reiterate at this point that what I'm saying is not a replacement for speaking with a qualified financial adviser. I'm merely trying to show you that even if you haven't quite found what you're looking for, there are still options – don't give up. If you do go down the path of cutting the budget back a little, remember it does not have to be forever. You might only need to make some changes for 12 to 24 months; your situation could always change.

If you really have no room to move on the budget and you can't earn any more money, it's time to look at how beautiful and close your new home will need to be.

In my opinion, what this really comes down to is what's more necessary to you:

- the size and style of living you have when you're at home, or
- how long it takes you to get where you need to go.

These are questions only you can answer, but the responses are important because they could be the difference between buying an apartment close to where you need to be or a bigger house further away.

So how do you make this choice? While there's no magic formula to finding the best option for you, there are a few things you can do to feel a bit more comfortable and confident about the choices you make.

The simplest way to get a better feeling of what's more important when you're choosing between beautiful and close is by going to open homes that fit your budget.

Physically attending an open inspection and walking around a home, taking in all the property has to offer, is so important when buying. This is something we'll discuss in more detail in chapter 6. For now, all I want you to do is stand in some smaller properties and ask yourself – and whoever else is buying with you – this question in each room: *how much will I use this space?*

You will know pretty quickly by looking around and thinking about your and/or your family's daily activities whether the home in question will make you feel as though your lifestyle has been compromised. Will your possessions and furniture be packed to the rafters? Or do you look around and realise you actually never really use the second living space in your current home?

The point is, you won't know for sure until you're actually standing inside the property. Pictures and video are great, but if you're about to make a decision as big as buying a property, you need to touch, feel and smell to really understand if it's right for you.

If you've had a look at lots of smaller properties and feel confident that a more modest property will not suit your needs and lifestyle, that's totally okay. It just means it's time to take the final step and start looking a little further afield.

For this last step, you'll want to pull out your phone again and open up the Domain app. Going back to the mapping feature we used earlier in the chapter, it's now time to zoom out further again and expand that little green circle. How far out you take your search is completely your call, but if you've already tried to adjust your budget without success and can't compromise on the size or condition of the property, this is your last shot at finding the right home. To increase your odds, I think it's best to expand your search circle as wide as is reasonably possible.

Your property search page should now be extremely long, as well as being filled with a whole different set of properties you were not looking at before. Sorting through your new list should hopefully help you find a beautiful property that fits in your budget.

In a nutshell

- Finding the right property will only happen when you know what the right home for you looks like.
- Utilise my wants, needs and won'ts and beautiful, close and cheap methods to narrow your search.
- Be honest with yourself about what's really important and what you just couldn't live with.
- Use your newly sharpened clarity to find the perfect property that's actually going to make you happy.
- Get off the couch and inspect some properties within your budget that meet your wants and needs.

5.

THE TRUTH ABOUT TITLES

If confusion is the first step to knowledge,
I must be a genius.

– LARRY LEISSNER

If you want to live close to a CBD or regional hub, you might consider buying an apartment, flat, unit or townhouse that comes with a particular type of title. These homes commonly include shared areas (gardens, stairs, structures and so on) and usually an owners corporation.

Owners corporation: the legal entity that manages the common property of a housing development.

If you're 100 per cent set on buying a standalone house, feel free to skip through this chapter. However, if you're even contemplating buying any of the above types of properties and are unsure how they work, please read on. This chapter will help dispel some of the myths you may have heard while giving you a quality insight into they ways in which multi-dwelling properties may be beneficial or inappropriate for your circumstances.

Apartments, flats, units and townhouses will generally differ from standalone homes in that they have a different type of title. There are four main types of titles you will find if you're looking for these types of homes:

1. Torrens
2. strata
3. community
4. company.

Many buyers I speak to have firm opinions about strata, company and community-titled properties. I've had people tell me, 'If it's not a Torrens title, it's not worth anything because you don't own the property.' Whenever someone voices such a strong opinion, I like to try to find out why they feel that way, and whether anyone has ever taken the time to explain to them what strata and community titles actually are. Generally, when I ask, 'Can you explain to me what it is you don't like about the strata or community-style title?' I'll receive one of the following answers:

- 'The extra charges and fees are a waste of money; you don't get anything for them.'
- 'You don't actually own anything; it's basically fancy renting.'
- 'You have no control over what you can do to the property.'

Exploring these comments is a great way of showing you not only the differences between the two most common titles you'll find if you're looking at multi-dwelling properties, but also the costs, restrictions and considerations you need to think through.

But before we get into sorting the fact from the fiction, let's take a minute to understand what each of these different title systems are.

Torrens title

The Torrens title is a government-controlled central registry of all the deeds of land held within the country. The system was first developed by Sir Robert Torrens after over 40,000 land grants vanished in the 1800s.

In very simplified terms, a Torrens title states that you own the land and the structures on the land; however, easements or encumbrances may still apply.

Easement: an interest attached to a parcel of land that gives another landowner or a statutory authority a right to use a part of that land for a specified purpose.

Encumbrance: a restriction a third party may impose on your property.

Strata title

A strata title property is generally a property that has several units within the same construction. Think of an apartment building with 50 apartments in it. If you own one of the apartments, you own and are responsible for everything inside the walls of that apartment. However, any maintenance on the outside of the building is (generally) organised by the managing authority (strata or body corporate manager) and paid for out of the maintenance or sinking fund.

Community title

A community title is a little like a combination between a strata and Torrens title. Generally, you will own a parcel of the land. However, there's also a section that is deemed 'community/common property'. This can be anything from a small garden bed out the front to a massive pool and BBQ area and a driveway.

Company title

This is where a company owns the title to land. Shareholders who have purchased shares in the company are entitled to exclusive occupation of a flat in a building on that land.

(!) **Note**

There are several other types of titles properties can have, but they're about as rare as a hilarious dad joke. Due to their scarcity, I feel there's not much point explaining them in detail here. However, if you would like to learn more about other types of titles, such as moiety or leasehold, then feel free to get in touch with me (or my team) through the contact section at **pizzaandproperty.com**. We'd be happy to explain if you do find yourself in one of these uncommon situations.

Title charges and fees

Earlier I mentioned this common pushback: 'The extra charges and fees are a waste of money; you don't get anything for them.' Let's unpack this.

No-one likes paying bills. I can't think of one person I've ever met who gets excited when their phone, gas or car insurance bill comes in to pay. Unfortunately, bills are part of living in such a wonderful country; it simply costs money to keep things functioning properly, looking beautiful and staying as safe as possible.

Before we start to break down the fees associated with different titles, I want to make one thing very clear:

Not all strata and community-style titles are created equal.

I'm not saying I'm a fan of one title more than the other, or that you need to buy a property with a particular type of title. What I *am* a fan of is the facts. Instead of us just assuming that all community and strata titles are the same, why don't we take a look at the fees and charges to reveal whether there is value in them – or if the property is being mismanaged and the owners are being overcharged?

So, where do you start your research into community and strata title fees? Remember when I said that almost all multi-dwelling properties will have an owners corporation managing them? Well, the owners corporation is legally obliged to hold an annual general meeting (AGM) and record and retain the minutes from that meeting. These minutes are a great place to start.

If you take a closer look you'll see that generally, the fees for strata or community-titled properties will be broken down into several different sections. As an owner, you may receive a bill every three months with a total amount owing, but if you look at the breakdown (which should be listed in the AGM minutes), you will be able to see where the money is going – and gauge whether the property is being managed well or if it's better to steer clear.

Example strata fees

Let's take a look at a hypothetical building, Property A, consisting of 50 apartments. To keep it simple, let's say everyone pays the same strata contributions and there are 10 apartments on each floor of a five-storey building. (In reality, the higher you are in the building and the more floor space you own, the higher your fees are going to be.) The building has no pool or gym, but does have a small common rooftop garden with a BBQ area for all of the residents to enjoy. Table 5.1 is a simplified example of the figures you might find in the AGM minutes for that property.

Table 5.1: Simplified example figures for Property A*

Property A	Quarterly contributions	Current total held for building
Sinking fund	$225.00	$51,486.00
Gardener every six weeks	$40.00	$2368.00
Management fees	$25.00	$1250.00
Stationery/postage	$4.50	$237.00
Common area electricity bills	$18.00	$900.00
Common area insurance	$60.00	$3000.00
Building insurance	$120.00	$6000.00
Total	**$492.50**	**$65,241.00**

*This table has been overly simplified for the purposes of clarity and ease of understanding. It is important to read and clearly understand the actual financial reports of the complex you're looking at buying into. It is the author's recommendation that you seek professional advice before making any decision relating to the purchase or sale of real estate.

Sinking fund: a pool of money set aside to allow the owners corporation of a property to pay for major repairs and maintenance.

At first glance, Property A looks like it's being managed quite well; there is a lot of spare cash in the sinking fund for when maintenance needs to be done. Also, none of the charges seem to be out of control. However, after we've looked at what's being charged and how much the building costs to run, we still need to take a look at the minutes from the AGM. In the case, after a quick read through, we learn that last year there was a $4340 payment put towards changing all of the lights in the hallways from 50-watt globes to 3-watt LED lights on motion sensors, which resulted in a massive drop in common area electricity bills. We also read that the owners corporation hunted around for a better deal on the building's common area insurance, shaving off quite a lot of wasted outgoings. There was also a vote to use some of the money in the sinking fund to install a new BBQ and outdoor kitchen in the common rooftop area. Three quotes would be obtained and voted on in the next meeting. This is all very useful information.

Now let's take a look at Property B. Property B is identical to Property A for our purposes. Table 5.2 shows its simplified figures.

Table 5.2: Simplified example figures for Property B*

Property B	Quarterly contributions	Current total held for building
Sinking fund	$90.00	$7198.00
Gardener every six weeks	$100.00	$5000.00
Management fees	$38.00	$1900.00
Stationery/postage	$15.00	$750.00
Common area electricity bills	$40.00	$2000.00
Common area insurance	$85.00	$4250.00
Building insurance	$120.00	$2000.00
Total	**$488.00**	**$23,098.00**

* This table has been overly simplified for the purposes of clarity and ease of understanding. It is important to read and clearly understand the actual financial reports of the complex you're looking at buying into. It is the author's recommendation that you seek professional advice before making any decision relating to the purchase or sale of real estate.

This property is being managed in a very different way. First of all, the sinking fund has a tiny amount of money for the size of the building. This means that if there is a significant problem that arises in an emergency – one that, for instance, costs $30,000 to fix – each apartment owner will need to immediately contribute approximately $456.04 (assuming the costs were evenly distributed). This may sound farfetched but, when an elevator breaks, it can cost a massive amount of money, and it's needed quickly!

In addition to the meagre sinking fund, many other potential issues stand out when comparing Property B to Property A. For example, the management fee is much higher for Property B than Property A, and it also has higher fees for insurance and electricity bills for common areas.

At first glance, Property B does not appear to be getting the attention it needs to be managed correctly. After a quick read through the AGM minutes, it's clear that there has been no discussion on how to minimise costs or add value to the building. The building also appears to have been using the same overpriced gardener for the past 10 years. It's also clear that only a handful of the owners are present at the meeting, and the corporation just seems to be going through the motions of merely existing and has never really improved or prepared for any future problem that may arise.

After looking at two hypothetical properties, alongside an overly simplified look into how they're being managed, I'm going to assume you would agree that there is quite a difference between the two as far as where the money is going.

I'm hoping you've just said yes. If you did say no, then maybe reread the two previous pages in a little more detail.

Strata title and Torrens title comparison

Getting back to addressing the original statement – 'The extra charges and fees are a waste of money; you don't get anything for them' – let's take a look at which parts of the charges you 'don't get anything for' in comparison to owning a Torrens title property.

Using the breakdown chart from Property A, we've replaced the total column with two different columns: Torrens title and explanation (see table 5.3).

Table 5.3: Strata versus Torrens title*

Strata title	Quarterly contributions	Torrens title	Explanation
Sinking fund	$225.00	Yes	General maintenance around the house will be different from house to house; however, the general rule of thumb is to put away 1% of your property's value for maintenance. You should be putting away $750 per quarter for a $300,000 Torrens title property.
Gardener every six weeks	$40.00	Yes	Unless you like the idea of living in a dust bowl, I think it's safe to assume you would pay a lot more than $160 per quarter for gardening.
Management fees	$25.00	No	NA
Stationery/ postage	$4.50	No	NA
Common area electricity bills	$18.00	No	NA
Common area insurance	$60.00	No	NA
Building insurance	$120.00	Yes	While you do not have to take out your own building insurance, you would be barking mad not to.
Total	$492.50		

* This table has been overly simplified for the purposes of clarity and ease of under-standing. It is important to read and clearly understand the actual financial reports of the complex you're looking at buying into. It is the author's recommendation that you seek professional advice before making any decision relating to the purchase or sale of real estate.

At first glance, your bill of $495 per quarter could look something more like $387.50 if you were to only pay for the services that would apply to a Torrens title property. However, if you were to pay for these services as an individual, you would lose the benefit of bulk buying service.

Think of it this way: if you go to the bottle shop and buy a single bottle of wine for $30, is it fair to say you would get it cheaper if 50 of your friends all put in for a bottle each? Maybe you'd buy the same bottle for $25 or even $20. Instantly, your buying power has been dramatically increased and you will be able to take advantage of a bulk buying discount. While there are plenty of positives to owning a Torrens title property, I feel that this is one of the positives of owning a community or strata title property that is frequently overlooked.

I want to very clearly reiterate: I'm not saying that all company or strata title properties are the best deal or superior. I'm saying that if they're managed properly, you may actually be surprised at just how much less they could cost compared to a Torrens title property. I genuinely believe the most significant difference is that you are forced to put away the money each quarter for a strata or community title property, whereas with a Torrens title, no manager is sending you letters reminding you to put money aside in your savings account for insurance, building maintenance or gardening. This means you're less likely to add up the cost of these things over the years.

So, in response to the statement about owners corporation fees being a waste of money – yes, sometimes that's absolutely correct, if the building or community isn't being managed properly. However, if you take a look at the numbers, you may find that you're actually getting stable value for what you're paying. It really is all about paying attention to the details.

What exactly do you own?

The second most common argument I hear against multiple-dwelling properties is, 'You don't actually own anything; it's basically fancy renting.'

I'm really not exactly sure where this idea came from, or why a portion of the general public seems to believe it. Let's take a look at it in a little more detail, just to confirm what you do or don't own when it comes to strata or community title.

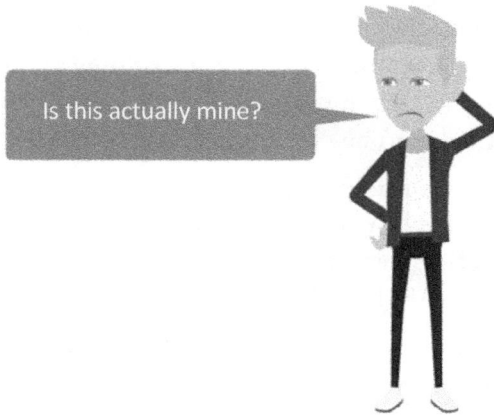

Is this actually mine?

Firstly, let me just say straight out of the gate that the statement about not actually owning the property is not true at all. When you purchase a strata or community title, you most certainly are not renting it.

There are some aged care villages, retirement homes and assisted living villages that have a purchasing agreement that's set up almost like a mixture of renting and owning; this is where I think the confusion may be coming from.

Okay, if you're a first home buyer or a family looking for your next home, why am I telling you about retirement homes? Just humour me here. It's important to know these things so that you don't get confused – especially when so much information about real estate is handed down from well-meaning family members and friends.

Let's say you're buying a property in a retirement home. It's a stand-alone two-bedroom villa in a community of approximately 150 other properties. There's a community centre, a pool, a gym and also quick access to nursing staff if needed. The asking price for this villa is $250,000, and the ongoing strata rates to pay for the upkeep of these excellent services in the community come to $500 per quarter.

Sounds like a pretty fantastic deal, right? All of that and a lovely new property for only $250,000 and pretty small ongoing costs, considering what you're getting for them. If you're feeling suspicious, that's good – you should be. The $250,000 price buys you the villa – as in the building and everything inside of it... or it might not even buy you that. In some cases, it may just buy you the right to live in the property, but it doesn't buy you the land that it sits on.

WHAT?! Yes, you read that right. In some of these scenarios, you do not own the land, or, sometimes, the structure. If you purchase a property in a place like this, the majority of the time you purchase a long-term lease to the land that the home sits on.

I want to make this very clear: *a general strata or community title is nothing like these retirement village setups.* When you buy a strata or community title unit in a complex – whether it's a complex of 5 or 500 – you will find the ongoing owners corporation fees are where the similarities begin and end. When you reach that happy day sometime in the future of paying off your mortgage, you will own a freehold property. The owners corporation charges will still need to be paid, just like the council rates or insurance on a Torrens title property.

Freehold property: a property title that the owner of the land owns forever.

I hope this has helped explain why there may sometimes be confusion over the ownership of a property when it's community or strata title.

Control over your property

Now, let's take a look at the third most common argument I hear about strata or community living: 'You have no control over what you can do to the property.'

Out of all the statements, this one probably needs the most consideration before you buy a strata or community property. Specifically, I'm talking about alterations or additions to your property. To say you have *no* control is incorrect but, depending on the size of the complex, your say about the building and common areas may be drowned out by the rest of the residents if there are conflicting opinions.

One of the significant differences between owning a house on a Torrens title and a property on community, company or strata title is the fact that you can do pretty much whatever you want to your Torrens title house (subject to encumbrances, or council consent for some additions or alterations).

If you own a Torrens title property and wake up one morning thinking that painting the front door bright orange is a great idea, then go ahead. It's your door. If you are sick and tired of mowing your lawn and would rather pave the whole front yard and look out to a beautiful sea of concrete every day, then go for it! Rip up the garden and pave away. Or maybe you like the idea of making a 6-foot-high replica of the Statue of Liberty that's also a letterbox.

Apart from a few unexpected looks and comments from the neighbours, no-one is going to say you can't do it, because it's your land. Unless the addition is going to cause harm to others or conflict with the council or legal regulations, then it's up to you what you do.

When it comes to community and strata titles, however, it's a little different. I think the best way to explain this is by comparing the titles to different types of government. Think of a Torrens title as a dictatorship – you own the property and can do what you like (within reason and council regulation).

When you own a community or strata title property, it's a lot more like a democracy, considering you're not the only one who has a say in how things should look or be managed. How the democracy works will vary between these titles and state to state. Every year at the AGM there will be all sorts of topics discussed and voted on by all of the owners in the complex who attend the meeting. For instance:

- Should we resurface the communal driveway? The cracks are getting bigger, and we have quotes saying it will only cost $3000 to fix. What should we do about it?

- Townhouse 14/24 would like to put up a verandah that borders the fence line of 13/24. What are the thoughts of the group? Should this be allowed?

- We have had complaints regarding barking dogs coming from several apartments. There has been a motion to ban animals from the building. What should we do about this?

These questions and many more like them will be addressed in the AGM every year. As an owner, you have every right to have your say. But just like any true democracy, your say is only as good as the majority. Even if you do feel very strongly about a particular subject, no matter what it is, you need to be aware that if the majority votes against you, there's not much you can do about it – you will more than likely just have to pull up your socks and roll with the changes (or perhaps lack of changes).

This is why I feel that out of all of the differences between the titles, this is the most important – because if there is something that you really want or feel very strongly that you *don't* want, the title could mean the difference between getting or not getting that. The biggest consideration that I would strongly recommend you think about is the rules around animal ownership. Having a pet live with you might be just as important as any other member of the family. Please be aware that some complexes will have a 100 per cent ban on all animals. Whether you think this is right or wrong is unfortunately beside the point. This rule can sometimes be the catalyst for unwanted conflict within a complex. If you do have a special little cat, dog or other furry friend, please, for your own sake, make sure they're allowed to live with you under the property's bylaws.

In a nutshell

- When you purchase strata or community title property, you do own the property; you are not renting.

- If you have any big plans of things you'd like to change about the property you're considering purchasing, consider speaking with the owners corporation management directly before buying, just to be on the safe side.

- Make sure you budget for the extra charges that will come in every quarter. While they may be a pain to pay, if the complex is being managed correctly, it could save you a lot of time and provide you with a better quality of life than what you would have in a Torrens title property.

🎧 Listen

If you would like further understanding on strata titles and how buildings are managed, listen to episode 67 of the Pizza and Property podcast: 'Before you Buy into Strata Listen to This – With Bryan Phillips.'

6.

WHAT TO EXPECT WHEN YOU'RE INSPECTING

The ache for home lives in all of us, the safe place where
we can go as we are and not be questioned.

– MAYA ANGELOU

So, you've narrowed your search down geographically and know how much you can afford to spend on your property purchase, and you're armed with an understanding of different titles if you're considering a multi-dwelling property. Now you're ready to get serious and take a look inside your possible new home.

This chapter covers what to expect during the inspection part of the buying process. We'll discuss the most common mistakes buyers make at open homes, how to avoid them, and how to give yourself the best chance of getting all the information you need without giving away what you shouldn't to the selling agent.

You'll hear the terms 'open homes', 'opens' and 'open for inspection' – they're pretty much used interchangeably. But where did the concept come from?

According to American real estate site realtor.com, the first record of an open home in the US was in the 1910s, shortly after the First World War. Before then, an agent would often reside in a show home from 9 am to 9 pm until the house was sold. It wasn't until the 1930s that agencies began to employ multiple agents, allowing them to take on more than one listing at a time – which created the birth of the open home as we know it.

The whole purpose of an open home is to give the buyer a firsthand look at what they're potentially purchasing, as well as giving them each a chance to imagine themselves living in the property.

Technology never beats the real thing

The technology available to market real estate these days is incredible. As an agent, I will often do 3D online tours that enable people to walk through the property room by room from anywhere in the world, as well as create beautiful marketing videos and interactive floor plans. These are all designed to draw in more buyers to every property and create a better result for my vendors. It's a fascinating time to be both buying and selling real estate.

As amazing as all of the new technology is, I don't think in-person open homes will ever disappear completely. While I have had a few people buy a property completely sight unseen, buyers like this are very much the exception rather than the rule.

More often than not, before a purchaser commits to buying the property, they'll say something like this:

- 'It just feels right. It felt like home when I stood in the kitchen.'

- 'Once I walked in the door, I just knew it was the one.'

- 'I could just picture myself having breakfast out the back under that beautiful tree.'

While a cleverly executed and visually engaging marketing plan is essential in getting the right buyers through the door, I can't see how it could ever replace the touch, smell and feel you get from actually being in the property.

How many opens should you go to before you buy?

How many is too many? Well, in my opinion, there's no such thing as seeing too many open homes. I know I'm a little bit biased on the subject, but seriously, I can go shopping for property the same way my other half can go shopping for shoes. If you think that sounds a little sexist, you should see our wardrobe – my clothes get one small section in the corner, and the rest is ladies' shoes and clothes. There's nothing wrong with a little healthy obsession – mine just happens to be in real estate.

While you don't need to have the house-buying obsession that I do, I still believe the more properties you look at, the better you get to understand the market. But how do you stay away from over-searching, or falling into 'paralysis by analysis'?

To make sure you don't end up with the same real estate addiction I have, I feel it's best to give you a solid number of homes to view. In my opinion, your average open viewings per house purchase should be about 12. There are two main reasons I've put this number as a safe amount of properties to look at:

1. It keeps your search concise, limiting you to about three to six weeks of searching (assuming you look at two to four open homes per weekend).

2. It gives you a good, varied look of the market without overloading your memory.

That said, if you walk through the door of a home and instantly fall 100 per cent in love with it, don't just keep looking until you've reached the magic number of 12 at the risk of losing your dream home. Or, if you end up looking at 15 or 20 properties before you find the right home, don't beat yourself up. The guideline of 12 is there merely as a flexible number to follow to stop you looking at 100 properties over the next two years and getting stuck in the searching process.

Looking at about a dozen properties will also help you spot the tricks some agents use in online ads. I've seen listings online before that have featured Photoshopped gardens that don't actually exist. The pictures showed perfect green lawns and flowers, then I arrived at the property only to see dirt and weeds.

It's the agent's job to offer their advice and expertise on how the vendor should present the home in the best possible light. A quality agent will do everything they can to make every property shine and stand out from all the other homes on the market, but at the end of the day, they can only give their advice; the final choice rests with the vendor. This is all the more reason to keep looking at more homes in real life; you may be pleasantly surprised how different they look in person.

How do you know when enough's enough?

There's another extreme I see buyers go through. It does not seem to matter if it's a first home buyer in their mid 20s or a 65-year-old couple downsizing, or even a young family in their late 30s looking at upsizing into a bigger home. This extreme is known as paralysis by analysis and it's not a state you want to find yourself in. Symptoms include:

- Continually missing out on properties that have been on the market for more than three weeks.
- Walking away from every property saying, 'If that one thing were different, I'd buy it.'
- Reluctance to put in an offer, even when all of your boxes are ticked.

- Only letting yourself really love a property once you see it's under contract (to someone else).

- Going to open homes at the same property more than three times and still refusing to put in an offer.

As well as witnessing this as an agent, I've been in this place as a buyer – and I know it's not fun.

I was in my early 20s, and I was looking at buying an investment property in the US. This was not long after the global financial crisis (GFC), when the housing market in the US was at an all-time low. I did my research, and all the numbers checked out – the economy was in the perfect position to invest.

However, for no apparent reason, I just kept stalling. Every time the opportunity presented itself to get into a deal, I backed off. This happened several times, and I was at a point where I was even beginning to get mad with myself, unable to understand why I was doing this.

A few years later, after having an accident on a drill rig and being unable to walk correctly for almost four years, I found out what was holding me back by speaking with a psychologist who was helping me put my life back together.

In the middle of working through the psychological issues related to dealing with my injury, we stumbled across the fact that at the time, I had a massive fear of failure. If I put all of my efforts into something and then it went wrong (like my former career did) it was terrifying for my subconscious. This held me back from committing to anything new. For too long, I let opportunity after opportunity pass me by and I couldn't work out why until I uncovered this.

I'm not going to pretend to be a psychologist; I can't claim to know how to smooth out anyone's emotional speed bumps. But, if you have any of these symptoms of paralysis by analysis, it might be worth having an honest conversation with yourself about what you may be scared of and what's really holding you back from committing to a property.

The reason I'm sharing this very personal part of my history with you is that sometimes, you don't know what's holding you back from getting where you want to go – all you know is that something feels wrong or scares you. What I know now is that the quicker you can figure out what's holding you back, the faster you can move forward and get to where you want to be.

I know this might feel like we're way off the topic of buying property, but I can assure you, we're not. The property market is at the whim of people's emotional reactions to situations. The better understanding you can have of your own emotions, the better a buyer you will be.

Once I realised the thing that was holding me back, I put a plan in place to fix it and made myself feel comfortable with what was standing in the way of where I wanted to be.

For me, it was all about understanding what could go wrong and then asking the question: 'What will I do if it happens?'

This simple exercise can help cut through the fear that may be holding you back from where you want to be.

If you feel this could be an issue for you, next time you face paralysis by analysis, sit down and ask yourself this question: 'If I buy this house, what could go wrong?'

Make a list of all the possible problems that come to mind, no matter how strange some of them might sound. Then, next to each of these problems, write down a solution as to how you could fix it if it happened.

Having a problem without seeing a direct solution attached is a very uncomfortable thing for anyone. But if you're shown a problem and can clearly see the solution at the same time, it changes the feeling completely because you now have a clear path to help you move forward. The only reason we're scared of the dark when we're younger is because of the unknown of what's in front of us.

So remember to look at about 12 homes in person so you can get a good understanding of the market you're wanting to buy in – but make sure that if you feel yourself becoming reluctant to make a choice, you ask yourself what could go wrong and what you can do about it.

Inspecting for value

Another big reason to attend more open homes is that it will allow you to learn more about the market in all of its details and unique differences.

Understanding a property's potential worth is more than just looking up sale prices online or using one of those 'accurate property price tools' – these can help, but they can also be far from 'accurate' in my experience.

Getting a real feel for the property will make a big difference to your negotiation power when you find the right property. Think of it this way: if you put in an offer on a home and the agent asks for more money because the house that sold down the road sold for $50,000 more than your offer, what would you say if you didn't know anything about the market? I think it's pretty reasonable to assume you might feel a little stuck. But if you know even just a little about the market, you may be able to reply with something like this:

> *Yes, that property down the road did have the same number of bedrooms and bathrooms. However, I inspected that property and could tell that the renovation had been completed very recently – it was immaculate. The renovation on this property, on the other hand, seems to have been done several years ago – I can see that there is some wear and tear on the kitchen cabinetry, the main bathroom has a chipped tile and the kids' bedrooms need to be repainted because there are marks on the walls. They're both lovely homes, but don't you think a newly renovated property would be worth more than this one that needs a bit of a spruce up?*

Boom! That response could have just saved you tens of thousands of dollars. Knowing simple little facts like this will only come with having a fundamental understanding of the market you're about to buy in.

When a buyer gives me an offer and explains that they came to that figure due to number 27 down the road selling for $700,000 and 123 Smith Street about two minutes away selling for $720,000, then proceeds to tell me a few details about those properties and how they compare to the home they're inspecting, I know I'm up against a pro. Basic negotiation tactics will be useless when an agent is against a buyer armed with real and substantial facts about the marketplace.

I really shouldn't be telling you this, but the truth of the matter is, understanding a market correctly is work – and most people either don't have the time or simply don't want to research a market because unless you love it, it's tedious work. However, if you can put in even 30 minutes of research, it could save you thousands of dollars off the purchase price by arming you with real market knowledge the selling agent wasn't expecting you to have.

Questions to ask the selling agent

Knowing *when* you've found the right home is crucial. It's very easy to keep looking for years, trying to find a 10 out of 10 home that simply does not exist. Once you've found a home that you think ticks all of your needs and as many of your wants as possible, you will need to know the questions to ask the selling agent to confirm this and set up your offer.

As a buyer in Australia, it's important to remember the real estate agent is paid by and works for the vendor (seller) of the home. Every selling agent in Australia has what's known as a fiduciary duty to their clients. This fiduciary duty *must* be upheld at all times.

Fiduciary duty: a commitment to act in the best interests of another person.

While an agent should never lie to a buyer, and there are certain things that must be disclosed, the agent shouldn't say anything that may cause a buyer to pay less for a property, or not want to buy it at all.

However, if you ask every agent the right questions at the right time, this will significantly increase your chances of discovering information that could help you negotiate a better deal on the property.

As far as I'm concerned, this is the best part of the whole process. Even before I was an agent, I loved going to open homes – whether it was helping a friend look for an investment property, or looking through hundreds of dumps until I found the perfect place I wanted to fix up, or even looking for my home I wanted to live in. It was, and still is, all the same. I'm going shopping, and I love it!

If you ask the right questions and pay attention to the details, this can be not only a fun experience but very financially rewarding.

Tick off your needs

When you chat with the agent, the first questions to ask are those that help you determine whether the property meets all your needs (refer back to the list you made in chapter 4).

Many of these questions should be answered by the photos and listing description. However, I feel it's always best to ask about any of your needs that don't appear to be met – you might be surprised that a property you previously thought was about to go in the 'no-good pile' suddenly becomes an option worth considering.

For example, about eight years ago I decided to rent out the apartment I owned and had been living in and move into a rental with some friends so I could save some more cash for investing. We all started looking for a house or townhouse in the city. Our needs list included having a bathroom both upstairs and downstairs – mainly because we didn't want to have to go upstairs to use the toilet when we had friends around. I also thought that the prospect of living with two other guys in their mid 20s sounded a lot more appealing if we had two bathrooms.

One day we were walking down the road towards a local pub when we happened to pass an open home. We thought, let's go for a quick look. My mate, who's also named Todd, said in his British accent, 'Oh, I've already shown you guys this one. It only has one bathroom. Let's forget it and get to the pub.'

It turned out that, while the ad was correct in that there was only one full bathroom upstairs, what we didn't realise was that there was also a second toilet downstairs. This is known as a 1.5 bathroom. As our good fortune would have it, this was not something the listing agent thought to include in the listing, and consequently the property had been sitting vacant for months.

It's easy to blame the listing agent in this story, and realistically, they were at fault to a certain extent. However, if I'd have had more initiative at that point in my life, I could have simply asked a question and been in the home I was looking for much sooner. If you're the one who takes this initiative, you may also be the person who snaps up the bargain because everyone else has simply looked at the ad on face value, like every other buyer. Sometimes it can come down to asking the simple questions that put you ahead of all of the other buyers out there.

What else should I ask?

Here is a list of questions that will give you a massive jump on a lot of buyers when it comes to sorting the right stuff from the fluff:

- Has the property had termites? If yes, was there any structural damage?
- Are there any easements on the property?
- How long has the property been on the market?
- Why is the vendor selling?
- Has the property undergone any renovations recently?
- What kind of settlement period is the vendor looking for?
- How many offers do you have on the property?
- Have any major crimes been committed at the property?

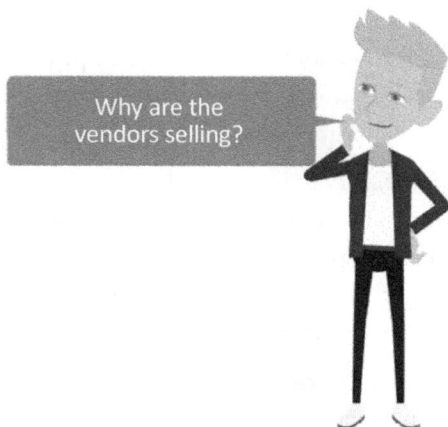

Why are the vendors selling?

The last question sounds like a bit of an odd one, and 99.9 per cent of the time the answer will be no. But for your own sake, you're always better off making sure you're not that 0.1 per cent, because it can be quite an unpleasant situation.

A couple of years ago, I was called out to do an appraisal on a property by a lovely elderly lady. Everything seemed quite straightforward, apart from the fact that the owner had only been in the property for about 12 months and was wanting to talk about selling again.

When I arrived at the property, I was quickly told why. It turns out that, unbeknown to the lovely new owner, the home had been the scene of a rather gruesome murder not long before she purchased it.

Without going into the detail that was given to me, let's just say a few disconcerting things happened in the master bedroom. Unfortunately, the new owner found out after she moved in. One of the neighbours popped over to say hi and said, 'I can't believe you bought the murder house.'

Naturally, my client was in total disbelief. Then the neighbour went on to describe the details of what had happened in what my client thought was her perfect new home. Needless to say, the excitement of moving into her home was short-lived after that. After a few phone calls, she was shocked to hear that the agent was under no obligation to tell her about what had taken place unless she asked the question – and because she never thought to ask, she was now sleeping in a former crime scene.

I don't tell you this story to scare you; I'm bringing it to light because it's not something most people think of asking. Realistically, the odds are so small it's probably never going to happen to you. But for the sake of asking one straightforward and quick question, it's worth knowing for sure that you've covered your bases.

The main idea behind asking these questions is to find out what you can use as leverage when you're negotiating your offer, and whether there is anything you need to know that may cost you a lot of money to fix.

The more you can find out about the vendor's situation and the integrity of the property, the better your chances of having some good negotiation points when it comes time to get the property for the best price.

Don't give too much away

Of course, the agent will also ask *you* some questions. What information should you *not* be telling the agent at open homes? There genuinely is a delicate balance between information you should disclose and what you should keep to yourself. Once you have an understanding of the difference, it will put you way ahead of all the other buyers in the market. Let's make sure we avoid being a buyer who plays the information game too far in either direction.

Some weekends I'll be running an open home, and I'll meet a buyer who will tell me everything about their life before I've even had a chance to say, 'Hi, I'm Todd, thanks for coming to our open home.'

On the other extreme, some buyers are afraid to say anything at all. They won't even tell me which areas they're interested in, because they think I'll somehow use this information to Jedi-mind-trick them into giving me all of their money for a property they don't want.

When I'm given absolutely no information from a buyer, it makes it just about impossible to service and assist them in finding the right home. It's like talking to a human brick wall; you can't help, because you have no idea what they want. Then that same person that gives out zero information sometimes talks about having no luck finding the right house and complains that no agent ever seems to care or help.

Giving the right amount of information to a selling agent can sometimes help you find a property that might not even make it to the market. Just a few weeks ago I met with a seller, and while walking through their property I said, 'I know just the person for this place.' It was a person who had come to a previous inspection of mine and communicated their wants and needs – providing enough information that I knew immediately when I saw a home that would suit them.

Long story short, I connected the deal off market and helped a thrilled seller avoid taking their property to market and an even happier buyer, who was over the moon with securing a property that was on offer exclusively to them. Without knowing what that buyer was after, I wouldn't have been able to connect the dots and lead everyone to a happy, win-win situation.

There is a healthy balance between the two approaches, which is precisely what we are going to make sure you have when you're walking through an open home.

Ready?

Is there anything you shouldn't tell the selling agent?

There is this common misconception that you shouldn't say anything to the agent selling the property. While it's definitely good to keep a few cards close to your chest, it can sometimes work against you if you are completely shut off to any assistance from the selling agent.

The real art is knowing what to say and what to keep to yourself. Most of this will be covered in chapter 7, but for now I'll give you a couple of responses and statements I hear from buyers more frequently than you might think. Remember, not everyone takes the time to read books like this and educate themselves like you are doing right now.

Here are some common things I hear:

- 'Just tell me what I need to pay. Is that enough, or should I write down a higher offer?'

- 'If they don't accept that, I could probably offer another $20,000.'

- 'Wow, this place is perfect; I'm not going to bother with another open.'

Any real estate agent would be thrilled to hear these comments, knowing they can move this situation to their vendor's advantage and achieve a fantastic result for them.

Imagine it this way. Pretend you're single and about to go on a first date. You're at the restaurant first, waiting at the table. Your date walks up to your table and says, 'Hi, I'm Sam.' Sam is incredibly good-looking; your perfect 10 out of 10. You get chatting and have a fantastic connection with Sam and think, wow! Not only is Sam incredibly attractive, but also seemingly intelligent and interesting, and is even making you laugh. You know you're really keen on Sam, and you'd love it if you could get to know each other further.

When you're getting towards the end of the date, do you think you'd be better off saying something like:

Sam, you're amazing! You're everything I've ever wanted. I want you in my life forever. Are you free tomorrow? I have a spare key to my place; do you want it now? Or should I get you a key ring with your name on it?

Or maybe saying something along the lines of:

Thanks for a great night, Sam. I think you're pretty fun to be around. We should go out again sometime. Have a great night.

I'm overemphasising this for comedic effect, but the reason I'm painting this picture is because I really want to highlight the importance of keeping your cool, even when you're incredibly excited and feel you may have just found the perfect property. If you show the selling agent too much enthusiasm for a property, I can almost guarantee you it will be used against you in the negotiation. There's nothing wrong with letting your interest be known – just do your best to keep it cool and hold your poker face.

In a nutshell

- Try to attend about 12 open homes before buying your property so you can have a clear understanding of what's in the market.

- Make sure you're asking the selling agent the right questions, to gather as much information for your negotiation as possible.

- Finally, and possibly most importantly, do not tell the selling agent you're madly in love with the property, because it will be used against you if you do.

PART III

MAKING IT YOURS

7.

NEGOTIATING TO
WIN THE PROPERTY

Let us never negotiate out of fear.
But let us never fear to negotiate.

– JOHN F KENNEDY

You've arrived at the 'pointy' end of the process and the risk here is that you'll get too emotional. Homebuyers intend to make their property purchase their home (rather than rent it out) and in a hot market you may have been looking at homes for a long time and perhaps been missing out. If you have finally found your perfect property after months of inspections, you don't want to lose it at this stage.

This chapter will help arm you with some tools of the trade that should improve your negotiating skills and increase your chances of getting your offer accepted.

Rookie mistakes to avoid

If this is your first time making an offer on a property, it might seem a little scary and you'll probably doubt yourself. The voice running through your mind might sound something like this:

- 'Did I offer too much money?'
- 'Did I not offer enough money? What if I lose it?'
- 'Maybe I should offer to shorten the settlement?'

If this sounds familiar, I hope this chapter will help improve your confidence.

I'm going to try my best to help you sidestep as much self-doubt as possible. I'm going to walk you through two key points to achieve this:

1. How to avoid the main negotiation traps set by agents. Understand what information you should keep to yourself and what you can give up without weakening your offer.

2. How to present your offer to give it the highest chance of acceptance. This has more to do with understanding the vendor's situation than just putting in writing what you may think is a good price.

So strap yourself in – I'm about to share a couple of secrets from inside the real estate industry that could save you thousands of dollars.

As a selling agent, I speak with between 300 and 500 people every week. About 20 per cent are sellers and industry contacts, while the other 80 per cent are people on the hunt for a property. These buyers come from all different backgrounds and experience levels. Some are first home buyers tiptoeing around with uncertainty. Others are overconfident downsizers who feel because they've lived in their house for the past 40 years, they must be a pro at buying property.

Unless they're seasoned buyers or professional buyer's agents, there's a general pattern I see a lot of buyers fall into once they've found the perfect home. They usually do one of two things: they go lowball, or they offer too much. Let's look at the problems with each of these.

Rookie mistake #1 – going lowball

Let's say you make an extremely low offer on the property, trying to grab a bargain because your cousin Barry is a 'property pro' and told you the home is way overpriced and you'd be a fool to offer what the vendor is asking. You then refuse to budge on your offer because cousin Barry told you to stick to your guns and show the agent who's boss.

In this situation, you'll most likely miss out on the property because you wanted to pick it up for a bargain instead of finding a win-win price that both you and the vendor are happy to agree to.

Let's then say you repeat this process on several homes that are perfect for you, continually missing out. After experiencing the same negative result several times over, you become very disenchanted with the whole buying process. (I can almost always tell when someone is at this point; there's a very distinctive look on their face that says, 'Please make it stop!') What was once a fun and exciting home-hunting adventure has become a chore, just like putting out the garbage or washing up the dishes.

Then, after your frustration peaks at your absolute limit, you put in an offer at or over the top of the price range – just to secure the next property that ticks the boxes so you can end the nightmare.

Unless you have the determination of Eddie the Eagle (an amazing Olympian from the 1980s; I highly recommend watching the movie), many disappointments are bound to get you down eventually – which is all the more reason to offer like a pro when you find your perfect home. An educated buyer understands value when they see it and knows how to increase their chances of securing it.

While there's nothing wrong with grabbing a bargain, it's best not to make a lowball offer at the expense of missing out on your perfect home for a price you would have been happy to pay.

In all honesty, the real truth of grabbing a great bargain in real estate is having another 5, 10, or 20 other properties you can happily offer on while having a care factor of *zero* if your offer falls through. However, this is usually unrealistic – particularly in a seller's market, when interest rates are low and there's a lot of demand and competition.

If you do have other choices, you can really negotiate tough and play hardball, but there's always a chance another buyer will show up and simply snap up the property for a fair price right from under your nose. No matter how accomplished your negotiation skills are, you have no control over that. Even if you're the best negotiator in the world, you can't stop other people coming to the property with a great offer and snapping up the deal on the spot.

Rookie mistake #2 – offering too much

On the other hand, offering at or above the top end is great for the seller, and may sometimes be necessary if competition becomes too intense. However, it's still the other extreme of making offers and should be avoided if possible.

Making an attractive offer

The process of actually making an offer might be slightly different depending on which state or territory you're in, and even which agency you're dealing with. When I first started selling homes, offers were always made on a standard paper offer form. Fast forward quite a few years and we now have digital offer forms that are texted to every registered person who walks into our opens. Over the course of your search for the right home you're bound to come across different types of offer form methods for all different agencies;

the most important thing is that you ask the agent, 'How are you taking offers?'

Just as a little side note: if an agent ever asks you to put your offer straight onto a contract there is no need to panic – I have had to do this with plenty of buyers in the past. However, if you're feeling more than those normal house-buying butterflies in your tummy, don't ever be afraid to say to the agent, 'Sure, we can meet up at 6 pm and put our offer on a contract; I just need you to send a copy though to me so I can get my solicitor/conveyancer to have a quick glance over it.' This way you're not cutting yourself out of a potential opportunity if everything is okay, but you're still getting the legal reassurance you need from someone in your team to feel comfortable.

Now, let's take a look at how you can make each part of your offer as attractive as possible to the vendor.

As well as things like your name, the property address and contact details, you'll need to fill in four main pieces of information on the offer form to complete a fully executed offer.

Offer amount

This section is where you write down how much money you would like to offer to purchase the vendor's property. The saying 'money talks' is very real, but it's not the only deciding factor in being the winning offer. As we discussed earlier in this chapter, your dollar amount must be attractive, but it's not the only part of your offer that matters.

Put simply: how much do you want to pay?

Deposit paid

The deposit section is where you write down how much money you can put down to secure the property. This amount of money is not in addition to your offer amount, it is a part of the offer. The idea behind a deposit is to give the vendor confidence that your offer is genuine and you have enough money behind you to make the deal come together.

Put simply: how much cash can you put down to secure the property?

Subject to

The 'subject to' section is where you outline any other specific actions or requirements that need to be completed before the offer can become unconditional.

Common examples include:

- subject to a building and/or pest inspection
- subject to finance
- subject to the sale of another home
- subject to the foreign investment review board.

Inherently, the more 'subject tos' you include in your offer, the more risk and uncertainty you're asking the vendor to hold before committing to the deal. Keeping your offer clean and straightforward can sometimes save you thousands of dollars because it makes your offer, even if slightly lower than other offers with more conditions, more attractive to the vendor. So make sure you're only including the necessary requirements.

If you think about it from the seller's point of view, who wants to hold onto another person's problems if they can walk away at any time and cause you considerable problems of your own?

Put simply: subject tos are actions that stand in the way of the purchaser's full commitment to purchase the property.

The image below shows the level of risk a vendor typically sees in an offer, depending on the conditions attached. As you can see, the most attractive offer a buyer can submit to a vendor is a *cash unconditional offer*. Essentially, this means that the buyer is not relying on a bank loan to fund the purchase; once cooling off finishes, the offer is unconditional and both purchaser and vendor can breathe easy. As we move down the ladder, you will see *subject to finance with pre-approval*. This means that the purchaser has pre-approval but not unconditional approval for their loan. While this may not be as appealing as a cash offer with no finance strings attached, it will still hold weight: it shows the vendor you have your finances in order and are ready to go with minimal delay. Moving further down the ladder, you will notice a common theme: each 'subject to' increases in risk for the vendor and uncertainty around the time taken before the deal will be completed.

Cash unconditional offer

Subject to settlement, all contracted conditions approved

Subject to finance, pre-approval already obtained

Subject to finance, pre-approval not obtained

Subject to sale, your property is on the market

Subject to sale, your property is about to go on the market

Subject to sale, your property needs lots of work before it can go on the market

Offering on property is not a science – it's more of an art. However, you can be pretty confident that the lower on the ladder your 'subject to' sits, the less attractive it will be to the vendor.

Settlement period

The settlement period is the time in between the offer being accepted by both the purchaser and vendor and the completed transaction: when the property title officially changes ownership from the vendor to the purchaser. Put simply, it's how long it will take for the property to become yours and for the seller to receive their money for the property sale.

The settlement period can range anywhere from two weeks to six months or more. However, the most common settlement period is generally around 30 to 60 days, or four to eight weeks.

Now that you understand what the offer comprises, you'll be better placed to start negotiating.

Seek advice from a conveyancer or solicitor

Now's the time to seek advice from a conveyancer or solicitor. You won't be able to avoid the paperwork attached to buying your new home, but you're not expected to understand conveyancing law. It's best to get legal advice when it comes to contracts. Your conveyancer or solicitor will help you with the 'subject to' clauses – remembering to only include the 'subject tos' you actually need, so you can keep your offer as competitive as possible.

In short, a conveyancer or solicitor will handle the documentation to make sure the property is transferred legally into your name. It's their job to check the documents comply with the state and territory-based legal requirements and to make you aware of anything important regarding the property. They will also make sure the payments are correct and made to the vendor, or vendor's financier, on time.

One of the documents your conveyancer or solicitor will check for you is the vendor statement – known in Victoria as the 'Section 32', and in South Australia as the 'Form 1'. There are different names for this document and slight variations in regulations and what must be included in each state; your conveyancer or solicitor will understand the state and local differences, and will help keep your purchase running smoothly and reduce the risk of nasty surprises.

If you do end up looking through the legal documents yourself as well, below is a general list of the kinds of information you'll be searching through:

- statutory warnings to the purchaser

- vendor's details
- title details – including size of land
- information regarding building permits issued in the past seven years
- details of any mortgages over the land (i.e. debts charged against the land)
- information regarding covenants, easements and any other restrictions on title (whether or not they appear on the title)
- planning information, particularly where zoning restricts land use
- information about outgoings payable by the owner of the property
- disclosure of any notices or orders issued by the authorities regarding fencing, road-widening, sewerage and so on.

This list is not exhaustive and it's important to get a legal review of all documentation before you decide to purchase the property.

Buying a property is likely to be the biggest financial transaction you make, so don't scrimp on legal advice. If nothing else, it will help you pass the sleep test.

Negotiation 101

The process of negotiating with a real estate agent can be a little scary, especially if you're not a very outgoing person. While I can't speak for all agents, I can tell you that the top-selling agents will welcome the new negotiation skills you'll be using on them after reading this chapter. They will be impressed that you're coming to the table understanding some tricks of the trade. The ace you're going to have up your sleeve is that the agent won't know just how many of these tricks you have coming to them. So play it cool, ask the right things and deflect the loaded questions so you can get your home for the best price.

My goal with this section isn't to have you walking away as a pro negotiator; my goal is to make sure you have a good understanding of the questions to ask and how to strengthen your offer while negotiating, along with the questions the selling agent may ask as potential traps. Giving you this basic understanding will undoubtedly increase your chances of getting the right property for the right price.

The way we're going to do this is by breaking down a series of questions the selling agent may ask you and the safe ways to respond, as well as listing some of the ways you want to make sure you do *not* respond.

I'm guessing at this point you're wondering why I, as a real estate agent, would be giving you tips on how to buy a property at a better price. Surely, this book itself is some kind of trap. Personally, I hate it when people say, 'Trust me.' When I hear someone say that, it's the quickest way to get me to *not* trust them. So I want you to read this section with an open mind and walk through it with your own gut feeling. I know the information I'm about to share will be incredibly helpful for you as a buyer, but it's not the only piece of the puzzle to being a great real estate agent – which is why I'm happy to share these secrets.

Think of it like an AFL footballer teaching you the best way to kick a football. They could share some tips and tricks that could give you a massive edge on your opponents and significantly improve the way you kick a football, but I don't think they'd be worried you're about to take their spot on the team anytime soon. There's a lot more to doing what they do than just that one aspect of the game.

Know when the negotiation starts

A lot of the time, the first part of getting a great price is knowing that the negotiation has already started. It doesn't start when you make your first offer – well, at least not if you want a good deal when you're buying a property.

A good negotiator will have most of the information they need before the offer is even made; so you'll need to learn the art of extracting information and protecting your vulnerabilities.

I like to think of negotiation as a game of tennis: every question that is asked can either be hit back to me with a skillful response, or it can be missed – the other player can't return the shot and I get the information I need to strengthen my side of the negotiation. Whether you realise it or not, this is precisely what's happening when you're talking with a good sales agent. They're continually trying to get as much information as possible and cause you to miss the shot.

You may not play tennis; you may not even like tennis. However, I want to use this analogy because it's easy to understand and makes the property negotiation process much simpler to follow.

It doesn't matter if I'm the agent selling the property, trying to get the best price for my vendor, or if I'm the buyer negotiating with the agent. It's always the same approach: hit the ball over the net inside the square and be ready to see if the other player can hit it back over the net inside the square.

Questions the agent will ask

Unfortunately, there is no 100 per cent foolproof way to win at negotiation. But by using these scripts to hit the metaphorical ball back over the net, you'll significantly increase your chances of securing the property for a much better price.

Let's take a look at three seemingly simple questions an agent may ask you:

- If this offer is not accepted, just so I know, what would your next offer be?

- If I list a property the same size but newer, would you be happy to pay more for it?

- What is it that makes you want to live around here?

These three questions, if answered correctly, could save you an incredible amount of time and money.

While I could write an entire book just on these kinds of questions, I'm going to keep it to these three. Once you have an understanding of how the tennis match is played, you'll be able to quickly pick up when a loaded question is coming your way. If you're ever in doubt, make sure you take a step back and play it cool; it could end up saving you thousands.

So without any more chitchat, grab your sweatband, racquet and ball, and get ready to start serving up some Q&A to win the game like a real estate Roger Federer!

Agent's question: *If this offer is not accepted, just so I know, what would your next offer be?*

Agents will typically use this question to see if they can get the price higher quickly. Sometimes it's just these 16 words that can be the difference between an extra $10,000, $20,000 or even $50,000 for the vendor.

Bad response: *Oh, I'm not sure... I guess I'd go up another $20,000, but that's it!*

As soon as you say this, you have just paid another $20,000. I am always blown away by how many people push their own offer up by sometimes tens of thousands of dollars in a matter of seconds by simply giving the answer to this question.

Pro response: *Yeah, good question. I'm not really sure at this stage. Why don't you just let me know what the vendor says first, and we can take it from there?*

Responding like this keeps you in control and makes you come across as calm and confident; you're not giving away any additional information, but you're also not shooting yourself in the foot and saying that's your best offer, which could also potentially cost you the home if another buyer walks in only $1000 higher than you.

Agent's question: *If I listed a different property that was the same size but newer, would you be happy to pay more for it?*

This question is usually asked of a buyer who has a friend or family member walking around the home loudly picking out every problem with the property. I find this is really common with first home buyers who bring Mum and Dad along with them to the inspection. The parents walk around banging walls, opening every cupboard and shaking their heads in disapproval in every room.

Bad response: *No, this is the top of our budget; we can't afford a newer home in this area.*

If a purchaser says this, the agent now knows that pointing out the so-called 'flaws' in the property is a negotiation tactic, because buying a newer property that is in perfect condition is not an option for the purchaser. So when they put in an offer with a long list of things that need to be fixed and heavy price overestimates of how much it's going to cost, the agent can take this with a grain of salt.

Pro response: *I'm happy to look at some different properties. I like this type of home, but never say never.*

This response doesn't give away any extra information and keeps the game open, with you calmly hitting the ball back over the net as cool as a cucumber.

Agent's question: *What is it that makes you want to live around here?*

Everyone's answer is going to be different, and sometimes not too much comes of this question. But every now and then, a buyer will provide the agent with a piece of negotiation gold.

Bad response: *We need to find a house in this street because Mum's just five doors down, and she needs a a lot of help around the home.*

Or: *The swimming centre is only down the road, and our little David is going to be the next Michael Phelps.*

It can help the agent massively if you give a specific definition as to why a property is important to you. If, later on in the negotiation, you then start using another property that's on the market to justify a low offer, the agent can respond that the other home isn't close to Mum, or the pool, or whatever else is really important.

Pro response: *I just really like the area. It seems like a lovely place to live/invest.*

Responding like this shows you're genuinely interested in the area and possibly the home, but you're keeping your cards close to your chest without ignoring the question.

Questions to ask the agent

Now that you have a basic understanding of how to sidestep some loaded questions from the agent, it's time to start strengthening your return shot. I'll give you a set of questions to ask the selling agent that will help you get the information you need so you can put together a much more powerful and attractive offer.

In precisely the same way that you want to protect some of your information when talking to the selling agent, you equally want to gather as much information as possible that will help strengthen your offer.

Most of the questions we're going to discuss should be answered by the agent automatically, but just for good measure we'll throw in a couple of curve balls that will more than likely be deflected quickly. You never know your luck, though; if you don't ask, you don't know.

Before we dive in, remember this important point: the selling agent has fiduciary duty to their client (the vendor), as I explained in chapter 6. In simple terms, this means that the agent must act with the vendor's best interests at heart at all times, without misleading the purchasers or directly lying about anything that could financially affect the new owner of the property. This is a very thin line that must be walked by the selling agent; it's probably best explained with a quick example.

Let's say my clients are going through a rather nasty divorce, and they need to get out of their situation by selling the property quickly. If a buyer asks me why the vendor is selling, I'd be a pretty lousy agent if I said, 'Well, their marriage has broken up, and they just need to get out quick.' I may as well put a sign out the front that says, *Discount house – come in and grab a bargain.*

Knowing this, a good agent will say something along the lines of, 'It's been a cherished family home, but it's time for the vendor to move on to the next chapter of life.'

If the agent responds in this manner, it doesn't give the buyer information that's incorrect; but it also doesn't undermine the quality of the sale and the value perception a buyer may have of it.

The reason I have explained what an agent can and can't say is because, whether you're getting the truth or a carefully scripted and diplomatic response, asking these questions should still point you towards some of the answers that you're looking for – which are the vendor's:

- true selling motivation
- true selling time frame
- true thoughts on any 'subject to' requirements
- true price expectation.

It's all about getting the information you need from the selling agent to make your offer stand out from the rest, without just increasing your offer price.

Every vendor's situation is different, and every property is different. This is why it's crucial to ask these questions first and understand the vendor's situation so you can tailor your offer specifically to what they want.

In the same way the selling agent is getting as much information as possible out of you, you're about to be armed with the right questions to start playing the agent at their own game. Let's dive in to the questions.

Why is the vendor selling?

This is a straightforward question that may not be answered in full truth by the selling agent. In any case, it's important that you note down the answer. Your reason for getting this information is to try to obtain a closer view of the vendor's true selling time frame and their motivation for selling.

Is the vendor after a short or long settlement period?

Asking this question will give the agent a chance to provide you with the vendor's true selling time frame. This is very valuable information for you to have, because you might learn that the vendor hasn't yet found their next home and would rather have a longer settlement – which, if it suits you, you can include in your offer.

Did the vendor do any work to the home before putting it on the market?

If a lot of work has been carried out at the property just before selling, this suggests that the vendor is putting their best foot forward to achieve the highest price for the property; therefore, the selling time frame may not be as important as the price to them.

How long has the vendor owned the property?

The answer to this question will help you determine whether the property is likely to have a high emotional attachment for the vendor. If it has been a loved family home for 30 years, you might have the opportunity to communicate that you wish to live in the property long-term and keep the rooms filled with happy family memories.

Has the property been an investment or is it owner-occupied?

If it is an investment property that does not currently have a tenant in it, this is a massive indication that the vendor might have a very keen focus on a quick sale – so putting forward an offer with the shortest settlement period possible may even be accepted over a slightly higher offer with a longer settlement.

How long has the property been on the market?

It will entirely depend on the market you're looking in as to what time frame is considered long. If your chosen area is rural, it might be common for a property to sit on the market for six months, so if the property has been on the market for two months, then it's not that big a deal. If you're in a metro hot spot where properties only last a matter of weeks (or even days) before being snapped up, and the property has been for sale for two months, chances are the vendor might be open to more flexible settlement terms. In many cases, though, it could be that the vendor is holding out for a higher, possibly unrealistic, price.

What's the lowest price the vendor is willing to accept?

If the agent has any skill or respect for the vendor, they will not tell you this figure. However, just like any profession, there are some agents who simply don't care – and if you are speaking with one of them, you may be able to get yourself some very valuable information to use in your offer.

Apart from the full asking price, what would the perfect offer look like to the vendor?

Not only will this hopefully provide you with useful information you can use when tailoring your offer, but it also shows the agent that you're human. It's easy to forget when you're buying a property, but there are real, living, breathing people on the other end of the transaction. Keeping this in mind can work as much for you as it can for them to help you appeal and connect to a vendor on an emotional level.

In a nutshell

- Your job when buying a property is to try to obtain as much information from the selling agent as possible to strengthen your offer, while hitting back any loaded questions with a cool and calm answer that does not give anything away that could be used against you.

- Consider your 'subject tos' carefully.

- Find out the vendor's true motivations if you can.

- Remember that the vendor is a living, breathing, and probably lovely person – this will give you a much better chance of securing the property.

- Create an offer that gives the vendor what they want, while also getting you what you want.

🎧 Listen

If you want to learn more about negotiating the best deal on your property purchase, listen to episode 75 of the Pizza and Property podcast: 'Negotiating Steps to Win the Deal – With Scott Aggett.' This episode goes through so many little tricks and tips that could make a massive difference on your property purchase.

8.

AUCTIONS:
GOING ONCE, GOING TWICE...

We don't see things as they are, we see them as we are.

– ANAÏS NIN

The majority of homes in Australia are sold in one of two ways: by private sale or by auction. With a private treaty sale, the property is advertised at a certain price (or within a price range). If you're interested in buying the property, you make an offer – via the selling agent – and the negotiations start from there. When the vendor accepts your offer, there is a cooling-off period (see chapter 10), you pay the deposit, fulfil any conditions you may have on your offer, and after that the offer is binding and the sale goes through.

The second way to buy property is at auction. This can sometimes be a lot more scary, because you are bidding at a fixed time against other interested buyers. Emotions can take over, and the advertised price can often be exceeded. As well as this, there is no cooling-off period if you buy at auction (unless this is a special condition).

Whether you love auctions or hate them, the auction process is something you should at least have a basic understanding of when you are buying your home. Imagine you've taken all the steps in this book: you've got your finance in order; completed your research on what you want, need and won't put up with in your new home; and you've found *the* property. It looks great, but next to the listing you see that terrifying 'A' word – Auction. In some states, sale by auction is the most common sales method. In others, auctions are seen sparingly. No matter where you're buying it's best to be prepared; this way, if your perfect home is selling under auction conditions, you are ready to take as much control as you can and increase your chances of winning the auction.

It's just another purchase

You may have thought that the quote from Anaïs Nin at the opening of this chapter was a little cryptic, but I really believe it's fitting. Realistically, auctions aren't scary at all. Sure, there's a lot of money involved, but I don't believe it's the high price tag that makes auctions seem scary. In my experience, I feel it's the emotions attached to so badly wanting to own the property and having no clue if auction day is going to end with champagne and celebrations or a drink on the couch feeling upset that you've lost out on another perfect home. While I can't give you a 100 per cent bulletproof winning formula, I can give you some very helpful hints on what you can focus on and control to minimise the feeling of uncertainty as much as possible, and hopefully help you change the way you view auctions into something positive.

The key to taking part in the auction process is to take out the emotion and understand the process. However, the auction process is designed to create that overwhelming emotional feeling: to sweep up buyers into making a decision they otherwise might not make. The drama is such that there are reality TV shows about auctions (think the final episodes of *The Block* when everyone's on the edge of their seats!).

So, let's simplify it. An auction is normally just someone standing in front of a few people using a range of different clever tactics to push the price of the property up and make you buy the property for more than the other bidders are prepared to pay. Understand what's really going on and you should ease your nerves and anxiety on auction day.

Be finance ready

Before you can consider bidding at auction, you must have your finance ready. When the auctioneer shouts (and they *always* shout) 'Going once, going twice, *SOLD* to the person on my right' (or left or wherever the highest bidder is standing) you are legally bound to follow the agent and a witness inside the property to pay the deposit and sign the contract of sale. That's only scary if you don't have the money to cover the deposit and the balance at settlement. If your finances are in place, as they should be, it's an exciting time – not scary at all.

Auction conditions vary slightly from state to state and property to property, but generally the conditions attached to your bid at an auction are as follows:

- The settlement period has been defined as 30 days.
- The contract is unconditional.
- 10 per cent of the sale price is payable on the day of the auction.

So tell your broker that you'll be bidding at auction and you need to have 'auction-ready finance' or 'fully assessed finance' approved. They will understand what this means and should be able to walk you through the steps accordingly. If they say something along the lines of, 'What's auction- ready finance?' then please quietly exit the room and find another broker or lender.

Do your due diligence

Buying at auction is no different to buying by private sale in that you still need to conduct a building inspection (see chapter 9) – even if you're not 100 per cent certain of being the winning bidder. (In some states the vendor will provide a building report, so ask the agent if a report is available.) In case you are reluctant to go to this expense, think about the greater costs you will face if the property has structural problems and you only find out when you move in! You really don't want that to be you.

Each state and territory has slightly different documentation that the vendor must produce to the buyer. This is the point when you should seek legal advice from your conveyancer or solicitor, to understand the legal documents relevant to the property. One of the worst things that can happen on auction day is if you're the winning bidder, but then very soon after find out the home has an easement running underneath that you didn't know about or a freeway is about to be built next door. (See chapter 7 for more on what your conveyancer or solicitor will need to check.)

Just as a side note, I suggest only sending documentation to your conveyancer or solicitor if you are very interested in a property. If you start sending your conveyancer or solicitor three emails a day on every property you might be thinking about looking at, you are either going to get a massive bill or your emails will start to go unanswered.

Registering to bid

In most states registering to bid is a necessary step if you intend to take part on auction day. This can usually be done on the day of or prior to auction. It's best to ask the agent what you need to provide in terms of identification – usually it's photo ID with proof of your current address and other contact information along with your full name. If you do not register you will not be able to bid, so please make sure you do not overlook this step.

Setting your price limit

To make sure that emotions don't take over on the day it is essential to set your price limit. In order to do this you need two things:

1. a very clear understanding of what you can borrow
2. an accurate idea of what the property is worth – both on the market and to you.

What the property is worth is irrelevant if it is out of your price range anyway. There's no point setting a price limit to stick to at auction if you can't get finance for anywhere near the right amount (refer to chapter 1 on getting your finances sorted).

If I show up to bid on the penthouse at One57 in New York City, I'm pretty sure they'll be escorting me out rather quickly once they discover I'm not really Todd Sloan the eccentric Australian billion-aire! Even if I know exactly what it's worth, I don't like my chances of getting a loan for however many hundreds of millions it sells for.

Please make sure when setting your price limit that you don't go over what the broker has told you is your maximum borrowing amount, otherwise your auction purchase could very quickly turn into one of the most stressful experiences of your life. I don't know many people buying their first or second home who can magically find another $100,000 in 30 days after getting carried away at auction.

You can get a good idea of the market value of the property by researching a list of recent sales (the selling agent should provide you with a list of recent sales in the area). Comparing all the sales nearby over the past few weeks and months can be extremely helpful in working out what you feel is a fair market price.

The most important thing to remember when setting your price limit is once you have set it, *stick to it*; write it down on your phone where no-one else can see and make sure you commit to sticking to it if the auction passes in or is held over. If you justify going over by $1000 you will more than likely justify going over by another $5000 and then $10,000 and before you know it you're way over your budget and locked into an unconditional binding contract. This is when the excitement quickly turns to terror.

Tips on bidding at auction

Here are some sneaky tips I've gathered over my many years witnessing, conducting and assisting clients bidding at auctions. Along with reading these tips, it's a good idea to attend a few auctions before you bid at one. You will enjoy the real estate theatre and get used to all the spectacle that is designed to distract you.

Slow down your bids

One of the main jobs of the auctioneer is to build the energy of the auction: the faster the pace, the more they can potentially push people into making split-second decisions that can sometimes mean an extra $10,000 or $50,000, or maybe even $100,000 over what people were telling themselves they wanted to pay for the property. Soon bidders are caught up in a bidding war and they start bidding way more they really want to. If you find yourself in this situation don't be afraid to simply stop bidding; pause and take a breath, and don't respond to the auctioneer who will be looking at you for your next bid. See what happens next. The biggest reason you want to do this is to break the speed of the auction, giving not only yourself but everyone else more time to think for a second and stop pushing up the price purely because you're caught up in the moment.

After a bidding frenzy, when it seems there's only one bidder left and the property has passed its reserve price, the auctioneer will shout, 'Going once, going twice...' then one of two things will happen: the auctioneer will either say the magical word, 'SOLD!' as the hammer falls down, or they will step inside to consult with the vendor. As long as the reserve has been met, nine times out of ten, when the auctioneer returns, they will ask for one last bid and the bidding may start again. Often this is when the serious buyers step in.

Smart bidders only jump back in when they feel it's looking like the auctioneer is about to give their third and final call. This might mean you're silent for five seconds, or it might mean you're silent for minutes – there is no magic time, as every auction and auctioneer are different – you just need to use this as a guide and go with your gut feeling on the day.

Throw in odd numbers

You might feel a bit silly doing this, and while most experienced auctioneers should know how to handle it, a good bidding tactic can be to throw in a few really odd-numbered bids. If the bids are coming in thick and fast in $10,000 increments, you could try bidding $8,750. It could throw off the auctioneer's rhythm just enough to break some of that fast motion they're working so hard to create. Just in case they do not accept a lower bid than the $10,000 increments they're currently working with, don't be shy about putting in a bid slightly higher – let's say $11,250.

Reaching the reserve

Often at auction, the auctioneer will proclaim that the property is now 'on the market'. This means that the bidding has reached the vendor's reserve, which is simply the minimum price the vendor is willing to sell the property for. This means the property won't be passed in and will be sold on the day.

What to do if you are not the winning bidder on auction day

If yours is not the winning the bid at auction, then I recommend two things.

First, tell the selling agent how much you loved the property, and ask them to let you know when a similar property comes on the market. The agent might know about something off market that they could show you through before anyone else. This is always worth a try in my opinion.

The second thing is to do something that makes you happy. I know this is a bit *Happy Gilmore*, but if you lose out on a few auctions in a row it can start to suck the excitement out of the whole process. If you lose your enthusiasm and energy for house hunting, sometimes you can become quite depressed and anxious that you will never succeed in buying a home.

If you have something planned for after the auction – a drink with friends, a long run on the beach, or maybe Netflix and pizza is more your style – whatever it is that will help you push past the crappy feeling, I 100 per cent encourage you to do it and get back on track. We all know there are plenty more fish in the sea – in this case, there are even more houses to call home.

What happens if you are the winning bidder

At the end of the auction, if you are the winning bidder, you'll have to stop jumping around like a seven-year-old who's just been told they're going to Disneyland because there are a few things to take care of.

At this point the agent should be walking up to you congratulating you on your new purchase and showing you the next steps. They will walk you through signing the contract and transferring the deposit. Please allow at least 30 to 60 minutes in your schedule to make sure you have time to complete the final steps if you're the winning bidder. I know it might sound obvious to stick around after the auction but I have actually had a buyer win the auction and then super casually say, 'Thanks, gotta run and have coffee with the girls – let's talk soon.' We had to gently remind her that we couldn't let her leave before the paperwork had been signed and the deposit paid (I'm sure her friends would understand).

What if no-one is the winning bidder?

If the bidding stops and the auctioneer consults with the vendor who won't accept the final bid, the property is generally 'passed in'. When this happens, the final bidder is invited to negotiate with the vendor through the agent. Often, this can be a great time to secure the property without all the noise and hype around you. Just make sure to remember all you learnt in chapter 7 on negotiating. I have conducted quite a few auctions on properties that didn't sell under the hammer but within an hour or so an agreement is reached on price and the property is sold.

Cooling off

Just a reminder that there is no cooling-off period if you buy at auction (for more on when cooling-off periods do apply, please refer to chapter 10).

In a nutshell

- Having your finance sorted and your maximum bid written down can help ease your anxiety heading into auction.
- Make sure you do your due diligence before the big day, and register to bid.
- Work my tips to slow down the auction and buy yourself time if you can.
- If you miss out, speak to the agent and do something fun for yourself. You deserve it!

🎧 Listen

If you want to learn more about auctions, listen to episode 32 of the Pizza and Property podcast: 'The Block's Damien Cooley talks Australian Auction Tips and Strategies.' We talk all things auctions and how to get yourself ready to win on auction day.

9.

BUILDING INSPECTIONS

A wise man learns from his mistakes;
a wiser man learns from the mistakes of others.

– UNKNOWN

If you've been looking to buy a home for a while now, chances are you've been speaking with friends and family, very excitedly telling everyone of your plans. As discussed in previous chapters, you have probably found that everyone has advice for you. One of the most common recommendations I hear is, 'Whatever you do, don't forget to get a building inspection.'

A lot of the time I think that family and friends, well-intentioned as they may be, can send you off course. But this advice, in my opinion, is solid!

It really doesn't matter if you're buying a brand-new home that's just been built or a rickety old shack that's 100 years old – a building inspection is one of the cheapest professional services you will ever buy in comparison to the peace of mind it should give you on such a large purchase. The only exception to this is if you plan on demolishing the building in the very near future; then it's a clear waste of money.

So, what's a building inspection and why should you get one? How much should you pay for it, and what should you look for to know you've found a good building inspector? All these questions and more will be answered in this chapter. But first, I want to start with a short story to illustrate the importance of getting a building inspection.

Do I need a building inspection?

A few years ago, I was speaking with a friend of a friend – let's call him Brad. Brad and I got to talking about property, and once he found out I was a selling agent, he was very eager to get my opinion on a home he was about to purchase. Brad was in his mid 20s and, having been extremely diligent with his budgeting, had managed to save a large deposit. He was incredibly excited, because he was about to buy a house for about $500,000. Brad very proudly told me that none of his friends would have a home as beautiful as his, and that all of his hard work and sacrifice was about to pay off.

After showing me the house on his phone, Brad asked me if I thought it was a good deal. I ran through a few numbers on the area and the details of the property, and I agreed that if it's the home of his dreams and he was happy with it, the numbers looked like they stacked up as well.

After he had finished telling me about all the beautiful and amazing features of his near-new home, I asked him what the building inspector said about the property. Brad looked at me, slightly confused, and said, 'Why would I get a building inspection? The house is only five years old. I don't want to waste my money.'

I said to Brad, 'Based on what you've told me, you've worked very hard for a long time to put yourself in the position to buy such a substantial investment. Why wouldn't you want to make sure it is a secure one?'

He told me that it is secure because it's only a few years old. I could see that he did not understand my point; I tried to explain it in a slightly different way.

'Imagine I was a stockbroker, and I said to you that I had a new company that had everything you were looking for in an investment for $500,000. You had the option to buy a report for several hundred dollars that would look at the details of the company structure and potential longevity to give you peace of mind that you were investing your money wisely. Would you buy the report?'

Brad said, 'Of course I'd buy the report. But this is my home; it's not just an investment.'

I agreed and said, 'I understand that this is much more to you than just making money; but in my opinion, that's all the more reason to get a report that offers peace of mind. If a lousy investment falls apart, you might be a bit sad or angry but you'll soon dust yourself off and move on. But if your most significant investment and home that you live in falls apart, that would be a much bigger problem, wouldn't it?'

I'm not actually sure if Brad ended up booking an inspection. However, the reason I'm telling this story isn't to know if Brad's house fell over or stood firm; that's irrelevant. The point I'm trying to make is that buying a home, for the most part, is an exciting time. When everything comes together, it's a great feeling. But while 99 per cent of transactions go well, there's always the chance that yours could be the one that goes horribly wrong if you don't take the proper precautions. You can never be 100 per cent sure things will go perfectly; however, if you neglect to take the simple preventative measures that should help protect you from the big problems, you're increasing your chances of inviting in a big issue – which no-one wants.

Finding a good building inspector

Many years ago I was stunned when I found out that in South Australia, you don't need any building qualifications to become a building inspector. Technically, you don't even need to be a builder. I know – shocking, right? This isn't to say that you should automatically discount a building inspector that hasn't previously been a builder; it's more to point out the importance of asking the right questions when you're speaking to a building inspector before employing them.

In my experience, finding a good building inspector is just like any other service role you might be looking to fill: you want someone with a solid referral history who can explain what they're doing and make you feel comfortable with the process.

Questions to ask your prospective building inspector

Here are a few simple questions to ask a building inspector before you hire them:

- ☐ Can you walk me through what you would normally check in a building inspection?
- ☐ Is there a certain type of property you are more familiar with?
- ☐ Do you check anything other than what's required by law?
- ☐ Do you offer combined building and pest inspections?
- ☐ How long does a typical inspection take you from start to finish?
- ☐ Do you offer a written report? How soon would I receive the written report after the inspection is finished?
- ☐ What are the most common problems you find in these types of properties?
- ☐ Are you available to complete the inspection during my timeframe?
- ☐ What do you charge for your inspection services?

You don't need to ask every single one of these questions; don't feel like you need to use this as a script, like an overseas telemarketer selling you a new phone plan. Some of these questions will be answered in the natural flow of the conversation, and others you may need to bring up.

There are also some specific standards you should look for to identify a quality building inspector. Let's take a look at those now.

Communication

Try to gauge the inspector's communication skills during your initial interactions. Do you think they will be able to communicate any issues in a simple and easy-to-understand manner? Anyone can point out a problem, but having the skill to describe what the issue is and what it could mean for you is something that not all building inspectors may have. I've met some building inspectors that are brilliant at explaining issues to the client; they give a clear picture of each problem and what it means for the property. Equally, I've also met others that simply say, 'This is broken,' and move on to the next point. For your own ease in understanding such essential information, make sure your chosen building inspector can communicate clearly with you before putting them to work.

How thorough are they in their approach?

Does it seem that the inspector will be thorough? Do they check the simple things, like:

- do the taps actually turn on?
- is the stove is in working order?
- does the heater actually produce hot air?

These three examples are actually not a part of the building inspection regulations; however, in my opinion, a good building inspector would be adding these to their standard list of checks and be assessing them for you. The building inspectors that do not check these items are not technically doing anything wrong; but personally, I prefer to use inspectors who do more than just what's officially required, giving me total peace of mind over the entire building.

How much should I pay for a building inspection?

Just like anything in life, you usually get what you pay for. Be careful of the cheap and nasty building inspectors. While I'm not going to name names, I have seen first-hand what happens when people have tried to save a few dollars and, in my opinion, potentially cost themselves thousands in future maintenance bills.

A building inspection for a standard three to four-bedroom home should cost between $300 and $600 and take around 90 minutes. Some inspectors may take longer, and some may get the job done in a quicker time frame, but this is simply an average for you to use as a guide. If you decide to include a pest inspection this will increase the time frame slightly, generally costing an extra $150 to $300 depending on the size and location of the home.

Should I ask the selling agent for a recommendation?

As I said in chapter 7, all agents must act according to the vendor's best interests, so providing a building inspector recommendation to the buyer could be seen as a conflict of interest. While you may meet some agents who will recommend certain building inspectors, I think it's best to err on the side of caution as a buyer and do your own independent research, choosing an inspector you feel happy with independently of the selling agent.

The selling agent's role is to be present for the building inspection and simply answer any questions they can when they're asked by the building inspector or the purchaser, should you choose to attend. If the selling agent thinks there is an issue with the building inspector or feels that they are not doing things the way they should be, it's not their place to say anything.

Beware of friendly advice

As I've mentioned many times in this book, friends and family can unintentionally hinder your property purchase when they are trying to help. 'My dad's uncle's brother's cousin is just going to look over the place for me' is not a viable alternative to a building inspection. It is something I hear all the time, and it always makes me cringe a little for the purchaser.

While getting your family member or close friend to look over your potential home may sound like a great idea, in my opinion it's fraught with danger. There are three main reasons to avoid having your family member or friend act as the building inspector:

1. You have no indemnity insurance if something goes wrong.

2. You may not have a procedure or checklist as to what is going to be covered.

3. There's a possibility of ruining a relationship if things go pear-shaped.

Think about this for a minute: even if your friend looks through the property with the best of intentions, and even if they genuinely are brilliant at their job as a builder or whatever trade they professionally work in, there is still plenty of room for error. 'What could possibly go wrong?' I hear you ask. Even if your friend is an absolute superstar in their field, if they don't conduct building inspections regularly, they may not check all the same aspects a good building inspector would frequently check, and may possibly miss something important.

I have personally witnessed friends and family members of purchasers conducting inspections; generally, they'll walk around the house for about 20 minutes, missing a lot of things I see building inspectors check. I can't help but facepalm a little for the purchasers.

If you want to your friend or family member to check out the property before you commit, I think that's a great idea – but using them for the only check is a hazardous move.

What to do once you receive your report

Before reading your report, it's important to understand that some building inspectors play up the possibilities, while others give you the facts. I have seen a few inspections come back with a sound bill of health, only to have the purchasers pull out of the sale because they've seen statements like 'White ants may be present in the area' written in the report. I urge you to look carefully at comments like this, because when you really think about it, they sometimes don't mean much. If the inspector found evidence of white ants in the building, you should 100 per cent be asking more questions and talking to the agent about what could possibly be done to fix the issue; however, saying white ants may be present in the area is like saying tornados could come and blow your house over, or there's a possibility that earthquakes may destroy the building one day.

Unless you have hired a psychic building inspector (which would probably be an excellent idea for a reality TV show), make sure, for your own sake, that you make your decisions based on the facts – not on fictional ideas of what could possibly, maybe happen sometime in the future.

Sometimes there are legitimate issues discovered during the building inspection that can justify changing your mind. If your building inspection report lists a raft of structural issues you weren't aware of that would warrant an almost entire rebuild, fair call – you need to ask yourself whether you have the skills, time or finances to deal with the issue. However, it's important to understand the difference between what *is* a scary problem and what just *sounds like* a scary problem. You need to make sure you're making your decisions based on facts, not fear.

While there are plenty of fantastic building inspectors out there, there are some whose business model is to scare you out of your purchase; this way, you'll make an offer on another property and they'll get your business again. With this in mind, please make sure that any problems highlighted in the report are real problems that can be quantified and managed.

If your building report does come back with a genuine issue that you feel unsure or uncomfortable about, I strongly recommend you speak with the agent first before deciding on your next steps –there may be something that can be done to fix the issue, or the price may be revised if the problem is significant enough. The state or territory you're buying in and whether you have a 'subject to building inspection' clause in your contract will greatly change the rights you as the purchaser have, and whether you can walk away without forfeiting your deposit. Make sure to always talk to the agent and your conveyancer or solicitor about your deadline to walk away from the deal and reclaim your deposit if significant structural or pest issues are found.

In a nutshell

- A building inspection really is one of the cheapest insurance policies you will ever buy.

- It's important to make sure that you hire a professional to conduct the inspection for you.

- Follow my tips to sort the great building inspectors from the not-so-great.

- Make sure your inspector has the skills to clearly communicate what the issues are if any are found.

10.

WHAT IF YOU CHANGE YOUR MIND?

Sometimes you change your mind...
sometimes your mind changes you.

– BINYOMIN SCHEMA

We all change our minds from time to time, right? There are many reasons you might decide not to go ahead with your property purchase – even after you have paid your deposit and signed a contract. This chapter discusses how long you have to change your mind – known in real estate speak as the cooling-off period. It also looks at how you notify the agent and vendor of your decision to exit easily and with no penalties.

Cooling-off period: a short period after committing to a home purchase where the buyer can change their mind.

Depending on the state or territory you're buying in, details such as the way your cooling-off period will start, how long it will go for and whether you are even entitled to a cooling-off period will differ greatly.

Why would I change my mind?

First, we'll consider the reasons you may decide to exit a contract of sale.

It might seem crazy that you would consider exiting your property purchase, after spending so long searching for and finding your chosen home. However, there are many circumstances that can cause you to change your mind about your purchase. For example, you may have had an unexpected family event happen in your life that means you can no longer commit to the property; or perhaps your boss called you just after you signed the paperwork and said the company is letting you go. Maybe you're one of those people who likes to go out and buy real estate without telling their significant other until they've signed the paperwork (yes, I've had that happen).

However, the most common reason I see buyers cool off isn't anything extreme or odd; it's due to something they discover during the building-inspection process (which is why I dedicated a whole chapter to this subject – you should read it, if you haven't already).

She'll be right (or will she?)

Cooling off is an area of property buying that you, as a buyer, should understand very clearly. Even if you think you've found the perfect home and there's no way you'll be cooling off, I still strongly recommend you have a full understanding of how the process works – in case something unexpected arises and you need to back out of a deal before it's too late.

I've dealt with a surprisingly large number of buyers who just assumed they understood the cooling-off rules, then came close to landing themselves in hot water.

I remember one buyer I was working with who almost cost himself a considerable amount of money due to his blatant lack of care for any details. It was 2017, and I was selling the strangest house I've ever sold to date. This partially renovated home had seven bedrooms and three bathrooms, and belonged to an awesome family who had relocated from Adelaide to Perth and were about to relocate again to Dubai. He was a photographer and she was an Olympic gymnastics coach – both extremely busy people who also had a young family, so time was a massive issue for them. Completing the renovation on the property prior to putting it on the market was simply not an option.

This property was so tricky to sell because it had a half-changed floorplan, it was on a half-sized block and had about 100 half-finished jobs that the new owner would need to complete – and some potentially significant issues as well.

I sold this property four times. I'm not joking: *four times* I put this home under contract. Each buyer kept cooling off for different reasons. Then, I met a buyer who we'll name Jeff. Jeff lived inter-state and was relocating to Adelaide with his family, and the seven bedrooms were a huge attraction for him. Unfortunately for Jeff, he was a nice guy but very overconfident in his approach. Whenever I tried to explain things to him, he told me, 'Yeah, yeah, yeah, she'll be right. I know how this works, Todd.'

Long story short, Jeff put in an offer, we negotiated back and forth and agreed on a price, and then he organised a building inspection. I told him from the outset the building inspection report was not going to come back perfect, as there were plenty of little jobs left to do on the house. I tried to explain the steps to take if there was a problem. Naturally, Jeff knew best, and just told me, 'Yeah, yeah, yeah, she'll be right, Todd. I've done this before.'

As you may have guessed by now, 'she' was not right, and Jeff didn't know how it worked. He was not happy with the building inspection report and wanted to cool off, but instead of going through the formal channels he sent me a text message that said,

> I want to pull out of the sale of [wrong property address]. Thanks, Jeff.

I tried ringing Jeff about five times, with no answer. The thing that Jeff didn't know, *because he wouldn't let me tell him*, was that a cooling-off notice can't be served via text in South Australia, and it must contain the correct address of the property you want to cool off from. Considering there were only six hours remaining of the cooling-off period at this point, and Jeff was completely non-responsive, I decided to send Jeff a text. I said,

> Hi Jeff, Your cooling-off notice is invalid and you will be committed to the purchase in six hours. If you would like to cool off formally, please call ASAP. Thanks, Todd Sloan.

Jeff called me back very quickly and allowed me to explain to him why his cooling-off notice wasn't valid. I told Jeff he should send me his cooling-off notice via email, from the email address stated on the paperwork – and that he needed to include the correct address.

(Technically, there are several other ways to legally cool off in South Australia, including providing written notice via registered post directly to the agent, or verbally cooling off directly to the selling agent in their office or the vendor at their home. However, while these other options are legal, I strongly recommend cooling off via email –it's the cleanest and quickest way, and also gives you an easy-to-find record that will protect you as the purchaser.)

As you can see, in this situation I did the right thing and chased the buyer to make sure he had the correct information. The reason I'm pressing on this point so hard is because it would be foolish to think that every agent would try so hard to get the right information to a buyer that wanted to cool off. There are some agents out there that would think, *'I tried to tell them – it's their problem now.'*

This is why it's so important to clearly understand whether you even have a cooling-off period and if you do, when it starts, how long it will go for, how you are required to cool off, and how your deposit refund works if you have paid a deposit.

Understanding the cooling-off process

As I said earlier in the chapter, it's important to note that cooling off works differently in each state and territory in Australia. Some states have more days than others, and some have no cooling-off period at all. Some states require you to put down a non-refundable deposit, and for others no deposit is required (until the cooling-off timeframe has ultimately passed).

Understanding the details of your state or territory's rules is one of the more tedious parts of the buying process, but it is undoubtedly vital and worth fully understanding. That said, I've only included the facts you need in this chapter, and I promise to keep it as short as I can.

To understand cooling off correctly and debunk any rumours you may have heard from others, we need to start at the formal offer stage. I'll run through a quick scenario that outlines each step of the process so you get a clear understanding of exactly how cooling off works.

When does cooling off begin, and how long does it last?

If you're buying in a state or territory that gives you cooling-off rights, you will need to have a firm grasp of exactly when your cooling-off clock starts and finishes. Figure 10.1 shows how long cooling-off lasts in each state and territory and the percentage of deposit you'll lose if you do cool off, and table 10.1 lists the triggers for the cooling-off period to start. This information is correct at the time of writing (2021) and should be used as a guide only; it must be used in conjunction with advice from your trusted legal adviser – not as a substitute for it. It does not matter what state you're buying in; the one thing that does not change is that you must always confirm your cooling-off rights with both your conveyancer/solicitor and the agent you're buying the property from.

Figure 10.1: Cooling-off time frames and deposit refunds

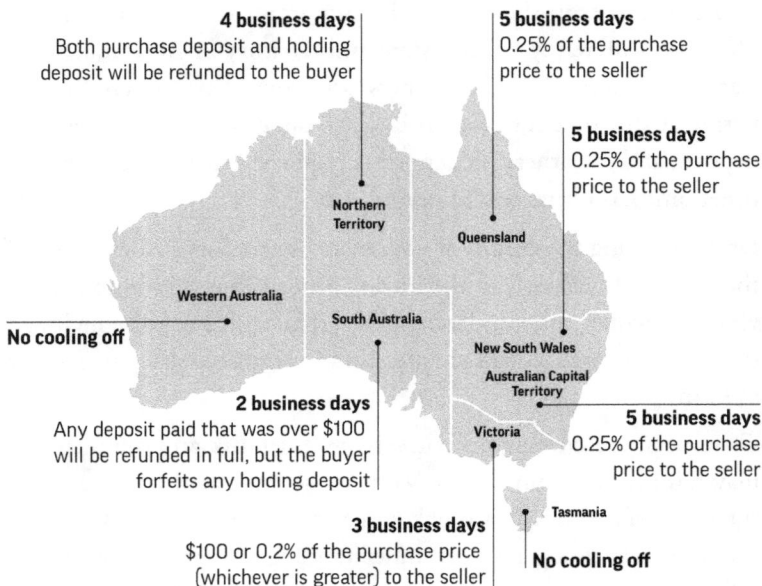

4 business days
Both purchase deposit and holding
deposit will be refunded to the buyer

5 business days
0.25% of the purchase
price to the seller

5 business days
0.25% of the purchase
price to the seller

Northern
Territory

Queensland

Western Australia

No cooling off

South Australia

New South Wales

Australian Capital
Territory

2 business days
Any deposit paid that was over $100
will be refunded in full, but the buyer
forfeits any holding deposit

Victoria

5 business days
0.25% of the purchase
price to the seller

Tasmania

3 business days
$100 or 0.2% of the purchase price
(whichever is greater) to the seller

No cooling off

Table 10.1: Cooling-off triggers in each state and territory

State	What triggers the cooling-off period to begin?
Australian Capital Territory	When contracts are exchanged
New South Wales	When contracts are exchanged
Northern Territory	When the contract is last signed by either you or the vendor and exchanged
Queensland	When you receive the fully signed contract
South Australia	When the Form 1 document is served, after both you and the vendor has a fully signed contract
Tasmania	No cooling off
Victoria	When you sign the contract, whether the vendor has signed or not
Western Australia	No cooling off

Can the cooling-off period be extended or waived?

This is a question I've been asked quite a few times. The short answer is no. The long answer is yes, with a but. If an agent tries to extend the cooling-off period through a change to the contract (the technical term for this is 'by way of an addendum'), this will not be legally binding. An agent has no legal right to either extend or reduce the cooling-off time frame. Like I said, there is a *but:* if the cooling-off extension is agreed upon and correspondence is made through both the vendor's and purchaser's conveyancers/solicitors, the cooling-off period may be waived – depending on what state or territory you're buying in. Make sure you check this with your conveyancer/solicitor.

So, what happens if I do want to cool off?

If you're thinking about cooling off, I recommend talking with the agent first before you make a choice out of fear that you could later regret. This is because the issue might be fixable. In the past I've had purchasers tell me they want to cool off and I've replied with, 'I'm sorry to hear that, do you mind me asking why?' Often the purchaser will explain that they're having second thoughts because of a particular problem, but once they find out the problem is easily fixed prior to the property changing hands they are happy to continue with the sale. Of course, you should also seek advice from your conveyancer/solicitor if you have any concerns. Cooling off should be treated as a last resort, not a kneejerk reaction before all options have been explored.

If you still don't feel comfortable with what the agent has said, always go back to talking with your conveyancer/solicitor for any legal reassurance.

Note that you are under no obligation to give a reason as to why you're cooling off on a property; so if an agent tries to tell you that you must provide a reason for your cooling off to be valid, that is entirely incorrect. With that said, out of common courtesy, I recommend you disclose your reason if you can. Cooling off can be a very stressful experience for the vendor, and sometimes knowing why a deal has fallen over can help them fix whatever needs to be fixed, if they can.

The way in which you must communicate your request to cool off is different in each state; they all have their own variations of what will and will not be accepted as a formal cool-off notice. For example, a formal cool-off via email from the purchaser's registered email to the selling agent is fine in South Australia, but at the time of writing, most contracts in the Northern Territory would not accept email as a formal cool-off.

Here is an email template you can use to communicate your cool-off in those states that allow it:

> Hi [selling agent's name],
>
> I [purchaser's name] would like to give my formal cooling-off notice on [property address].
>
> Unfortunately, because of [insert reason], I/we will no longer be able to proceed with the purchase of [property address].
>
> Best of luck with the sale.
>
> Regards,
>
> [Purchaser's name]
> [Purchaser's contact number]

What if I change my mind *again*?

So, what happens if you request to cool off but then your circumstances change and you decide you do want to buy the property after all?

Let me tell you about a situation I see all too often. The buyer receives their building inspection report, becomes scared from what's been said, then cools off before speaking with me about a possible resolution. As a selling agent, as soon as I receive a formal cooling-off notice from a buyer I go back into full-on sales mode – working as hard as possible to get the property back under contract with another purchaser. This can be achieved very quickly, especially if there are several other people who have made offers on the property. Sometimes, the original interested buyer will then call back and say, 'I've spoken with my partner and we want to take back our cool-off and buy the home.' This is one of the few parts of my job that I don't like because, at this point, I have to tell them that the property is back under contract – and even if they were to change their offer, the vendor is now contractually obliged to continue with the new purchaser.

This is why it's so important to think clearly about the situation and explore possible solutions with the selling agent and your conveyancer/solicitor before you cool off – because once you've cooled off, there is no 'uncool-off' button you can push.

In a nutshell

- Check your state or territory government website and speak with your conveyancer/solicitor to make sure you understand how cooling off works in the area you want to purchase in.

- Cooling off should always be used as an absolute last resort.

- If you do feel you need to cool off, always speak with the agent to work out whether the issue can be resolved.

- Make sure you formally cool off using the advice given to you from your trusted conveyancer/solicitor so you can sleep easy.

🎧 Listen

If you want to learn more about cooling off in your state or territory, listen to episode 81 of the Pizza and Property podcast: 'Cooling Off Around the Country.' We talk with legal professionals in each state about how it works and if there are any simple differences you need to be aware of.

11.

SETTLEMENT AND
MOVING IN

When you write things down, you commit to doing them.
If you simply tell me what you want to do, there is really
no commitment in getting things done.

– DAVID COTTRELL

Getting to this point means you've already accomplished an incredible amount. I want you to feel proud of yourself for putting all of the steps in place to achieve the Great Australian Dream of owning a home.

When you get to this stage, it's easy to forget just how many steps you've taken to put yourself ahead of the pack and get to where you want. With that said, I want to break it down, just to help you appreciate how awesome you are right now!

So far, you've managed to:

- get all of your finances in order (which is no easy task)
- find a broker who has helped you navigate your way through the banks and find a fantastic deal on your loan

- decide what and where the perfect property is (probably the hardest part)
- look at hundreds of properties online (or maybe even thousands if you're anything like me!)
- give up your weekends to walk through many, many open homes and private inspections, which means you've got a whole heap of drinks with friends and time with the family to catch up on
- tangle with real estate agents and negotiate a great price on your new home
- do one of the scariest things in real estate: sign contracts on your new property
- organise and read your building report to make sure your new home or investment is solid one
- pass your cooling-off period.

Even though you're not 100 per cent finished, I think it's totally time to have a little mini-celebration, so pop some champagne, have the fanciest scotch you can find, or treat yourself to a fantastic dessert. You really have earned it!

What to expect during the settlement period

The settlement period is generally considered to be the time between having a fully signed contract (the technical term is 'fully executed contract') and the official exchange of names on the title. It's basically the period when the property starts moving through the motions from belonging to the vendor to becoming your property.

Settlement is when your lender transfers the balance of the funds to the vendor and in exchange you receive the deeds to the house (or your lender does, until you have paid the mortgage off). Once settlement occurs, you can pick up the keys and move in.

The following quote from a settlement agency in Western Australia is the best way I've seen settlement explained:

> *Property settlement is the process of transferring property from one owner to another. Although the aim of property settlement is simple, regulations and compulsory procedures mean that the settlement process itself is complex and time-consuming.*

It's important to note that due to the different 'subject tos' that can be written into sales contracts (see chapter 7), most settlements are slightly different in terms of precisely what needs to be completed, as well as the actions that need to be fulfilled before everything is complete.

While typical settlement periods run from between 30 and 60 days, a settlement period can sometimes run for much longer. Occasionally I will draw up a contract for a 90-day settlement; the most extended settlement I've ever done has been 120 days long. Theoretically, there is no set time frame as to how long a settlement is allowed to run for. As long as both parties in the contract agree to the duration, a settlement period could technically run for years.

If you do have a contract variation, a 'subject to' or anything you don't understand in your contract, best to get in touch with your conveyancer/solicitor.

While you don't need to be a pro understanding every legal and administrative detail (that's your conveyancer/solicitor's job), I strongly recommend having at least a basic understanding of the process and how it should flow – as well as what needs to be done and by who. Having this knowledge means you can sit back and feel confident that your new property will be yours when it should be.

The settlement guide in this chapter is broken up into three separate categories. This will give you a clearer picture of what to do and when to do it throughout your settlement period.

Packing for your move, organising who needs to do what and when they need to do it, and lastly, checking that everyone is doing what they're supposed to do, are the three main things you need to do to help make your settlement run smoothly. So just remember these three simple words: pack, organise, check.

Pack

Packing up your current home has to be one of the more annoying parts of buying a new home. However, it is entirely essential (unless you've just purchased an investment property, then you can skip this section altogether).

To make this process as easy as possible, I recommend packing your home in three separate stages: cupboards and shelves, keepsakes and large furniture.

Packing cupboards, drawers and shelves

In my opinion, packing these areas first is the best way to start moving, because it gives you a chance to get rid of all of the smaller bits and pieces that make a house a home, but aren't generally used daily. If you can set aside packing time for about one to two hours after work each day, it will take a considerable amount of stress off of your plate for the rest of the move.

Start by making a list of all the cupboards, dressers, cabinets, drawers and anywhere else you keep your stuff. Now put a checkbox next to it, so you can make it nice and clear how much you have done and what's left to do. Your list might look like this:

- ☐ Tallboy in bedroom
- ☐ Bedside tables in bedroom
- ☐ Laundry cabinet
- ☐ Kitchen cupboards
- ☐ Bathroom cupboards
- ☐ Bookcase in living room

When you're packing up cupboards and shelves, make sure you ask yourself a straightforward question: *do I use this every day or every week?* If the answer is 'every day', then leave it aside to be packed later. Otherwise, people are not going to be impressed when you stop washing your clothes and brushing your teeth because Todd Sloan said to pack everything in the cupboards first and, well, your toothbrush is in a box now, along with all of the washing powder.

When you're packing everything into boxes, it seems logical to simply grab any random boxes you can get your hands on, but one tip I was given years ago is to use all the same size boxes. This does mean you will need to buy the boxes instead of just using whatever you have around the house or have been given from friends and family, but there is a good reason behind this. When you go to pack the moving truck, if you have 50 different sizes and shapes of boxes to try to fit into the truck, it turns into a terrible game of Tetris. You'll sometimes lose a massive amount of space, possibly resulting in you needing to pay for another trip. I'm not a fan of spending money when it's not required, but if spending $50 or $100 on boxes can potentially save you $200, $300 or possibly even more in removalist fees, I think it's money well invested. Also, if you purchase good-quality boxes designed especially for moving they're likely to be much stronger than those you've picked up for free at Bunnings, potentially saving you from a moving-day disaster.

Packing keepsakes

If you have lived in a property for a long time, please do not underestimate how long packing up mementos might take. You might take an extra 30 to 60 minutes on each box when you start sorting through old treasures you haven't seen in years, or sometimes decades – especially when it comes to things like old childhood trophies and baby clothes. If there's a large emotional attachment, you can find yourself walking very slowly down memory lane, reminiscing through each box of memories from when you were little, or maybe when your grandparents were young.

If you have massive self-discipline and are a very logical person, then you will be fine. However, if you cried during the first 20 minutes of

The Lion King, chances are you'll need to give yourself extra time to go through the sentimental items in your house.

If you know there's a place in your home where all of the special items are kept, even if it is in a cupboard or a drawer, make sure you don't pack this area too early in the process; leave it until you've completed the first stage and have all your cupboards, drawers and shelves finished. This way, if something happens during settlement and you need to pick up the pace, you've already got the majority of the time-consuming work done.

Now, once everything is packed and boxed up, what do you do with all of the boxes sitting around the house? You may be able to leave them in a spare room, or maybe take them to a friend's house close to your new home. Either way, once they're packed, you can already start to feel a lot more comfortable, knowing that a massive part of your work is now complete.

Packing large items and furniture

Now it's time for the big stuff! Moving your fridge, washing machine and other large pieces of furniture is no easy task. If you're the kind of person who smashes the gym every day, then maybe you're looking forward to showing off some of your strength – throwing the washing machine under one arm and a fridge under the other. On the other hand, if you're an average human, tall, short, thin, fat or anything in between, you're probably going to want some help with making a move – especially if you're moving from or to a house with a steep driveway or a lot of stairs.

It's definitely worth taking a quick look at your budget to see if you have some money available to invest in getting professional removalists. Getting a professional in to help move at least the large items will not only make your life a lot less stressful, but it should also streamline the process – getting you into your new home quicker, and literally taking a load off of your shoulders.

Organise

The organise stage is about sticking to and following the checklist to make sure everyone involved in the sale is doing what they should do when they should do it. The real trick with organising is just knowing who to make contact with and when, and what to ask.

Some of the trades and professions I mention here are optional and may not apply to your settlement situation. However, I've kept them in just in case you do decide to use them. I've focused on making sure everything is done correctly, not on shopping around and getting the best deal.

Here is a list of all the people you may want to talk with, and what you should ask each one:

Removalist

- What date(s) do you need them to come, and are they available?
- What time can they arrive on the day?
- Do you have any extra-heavy items (e.g., a pool table, piano, sculptures or garden items) that may need to be considered?
- How many workers do they have coming on the day?
- How many hours do they think it should take?
- What is their cost per hour?
- Do they take large appliances and furniture upstairs, or is it a door delivery?
- Do you need any parking permits or traffic permission? (If you're moving into a CBD and potentially blocking traffic.)

Conveyancer/solicitor

- When do you need to do the ID check, and how is this done?
- What paperwork does the conveyancer/solicitor need from you?

- When do they need you to come in and sign the paperwork?
- Is there anything unusual you need to know about?
- Are there any issues you need to be aware of?
- Have all mortgage discharge documents been completed and sent?

Broker/lender

- What paperwork do they need you to sign?
- Have they asked for any other documentation?
- When are you expecting to get formal finance approval?

Selling agent

- Will they make a time with you to put up the under contract sticker?
- Will they make a time with you to put up the sold sticker?
- When will key handover happen?
- Has the vendor completed any necessary works?
- Will the power be turned off at the mains on settlement day? (If needed.)

Services

- Have you organised disconnect and reconnect with your gas, electricity and internet providers?
- Have you notified your insurance company?
- Have you organised mail redirection?
- Have you changed your mailing address on frequently used websites?

Check

Checking is speedy and straightforward to do, but please make sure you don't overlook any of the checking steps. Just because they're easy doesn't mean they're unimportant. As the late former Prime Minister of Australia, Bob Hawke, once said: 'The things that are the most important don't always scream the loudest.'

I think that's very fitting for this section of the book: when you're almost at the end of something as big as buying a property, it's very easy to only pay attention to the things that are loud or obvious. But that doesn't always mean the quiet and simple things are not incredibly important; if left unattended to, they can create some massive headaches.

It's sometimes the most straightforward little issue that, when overlooked, can cause that most significant and costly delays during settlement. When one person in the line of settlement drops the ball and doesn't pick it back up, it can cause an adverse chain reaction that throws off the rest of the process.

When you make this series of easy but well-timed phone calls, emails and/or text messages, you will greatly increase your chances of helping make the settlement flow quickly and be hassle-free.

In my opinion, a lot of what you can do as a purchaser is straightforward, but it's rarely appropriately explained.

In essence, you want to make contact at the right time to all of the people in the 'organise' list to make sure they're still on track. It really isn't complicated; you don't even need to call people if you'd prefer not to. You can send a quick email or text message, simply stating something like:

> *Hi Todd,*
>
> *Hope you're well.*
>
> *Just wanted to make sure that you're still confident key handover for 123 Smith Street will happen on 15 April at 2:00 pm.*
>
> *Are we still meeting at your office?*
>
> *Thanks,*
>
> *Jenny Doe*

I've put together a simple timeline that you can follow during your checking process (table 11.1). Just look through the timeline and send the key people a check or reminder three business days before each deadline. Generally speaking, the steps outlined in days one to seven can be done entirely in one day, or they can be spread out over the week – as long as they're done in that week.

Ideally, all the tasks listed in the 'checking' column, and even the majority of the organising column, should be done by the respective business without you having to check in. However, we don't live in a world where everything runs 100 per cent perfectly all the time; sometimes a company may drop the ball or just assume something that should not be assumed. This is why being active or, at the very least, having a simple understanding of what to expect is extremely important – because if one of the steps is missed, you can very quickly and easily make the call or email you need to bring everything back on track effortlessly.

Table 11.1: Checking timeline

Week 1	
Day 1	☐ Make list of all the cupboards, drawers and shelves in your current home.
	☐ Contact insurance company and organise correct insurance for the new property, if not already done.
	☐ Contact broker/lender; make sure they have a copy of the contract of sale.
	☐ Contact selling agent to ask if the deposit has been received.
Day 2	☐ Start packing up one cupboard, shelf or drawer at a time and label each box with what's inside.
	☐ Contact removalists; organise quotes for moving.
Day 3	☐ Continue packing cupboards, shelves and drawers.
	☐ Contact conveyancer/solicitor and ask what paperwork they need from you and what documents you need to sign.
Day 4	☐ Continue packing cupboards, shelves and drawers.
	☐ Contact broker to ask if there is any other paperwork you need to sign, approve or view. Check if the authority to discharge your current mortgage has been completed.
Days 5 to 7	☐ Continue packing cupboards, shelves and drawers.
Week 2	
Day 8	☐ Start going through your keepsakes; make sure you have at least a few hours set aside for this as you may find something that takes you down memory lane for a while.
	☐ Go through your removalist quotes and choose the company you're happy with.
	☐ Call removalist and book in a date and time.
	☐ Contact your broker to find out how the approval process is going and whether the lender needs anything new from you.
Days 9 to 14	☐ Continue packing keepsake items and any leftover drawers, cupboards and shelves.

Week 3	
Day 15	☐ Contact conveyancer/solicitor and organise a time for ID check, if necessary.
	☐ Contact your broker to find out if finance has been unconditionally approved. (Conditional approval will not give you the reassurance you need; it must be unconditional approval.)
Days 16 to 18	☐ If unconditional approval has been obtained, begin moving any larger items if you have another place to store them until settlement.
	☐ Otherwise, wait until settlement day to move larger items.
Days 19 to 21	☐ Contact selling agent to organise a time and place for key handover.
	☐ If you're selling your current home, call your selling agent to organise key drop off place and time.
Week 4	
Day 22	☐ Contact conveyancer/solicitor and organise a time to do the final meeting and sign the last of the paperwork.
	☐ If your finance wasn't unconditionally approved when you checked earlier, check with the broker again.
Day 23	☐ Check with conveyancer/solicitor what time settlement is booked in for.
Days 24 to 28	☐ Start preparing any large items that are being moved that may need to be dismantled.
	☐ Contact removalist, make sure there is no double booking for your settlement day and book in a solid time that you have agreed upon with the selling agent and conveyancer.
Day 28	☐ Contact selling agent, check key handover time and place is still going ahead.
Settlement day	

In a nutshell

- I know this all may seem like a lot of effort, but if you follow these simple checks and procedures, you'll have a much better chance of enjoying a smooth settlement that results in you getting into your new home when you should.

- Make sure you pack your home correctly, organise what needs to be organised, and then check everyone is doing what they're supposed to be doing when they should be doing it.

CONGRATULATIONS

CONGRATULATIONS!
YOU OWN A PROPERTY!

You've done it! You are now the proud owner of your very own home. I don't think I can overstate this enough: you have now achieved one of the life goals of millions of people by becoming a property owner.

Depending on what you have bought, your new property might need TLC from you over the coming years. Make sure you keep on top of all the little things a property owner should, and take good care of your new home, because you've worked very hard for it.

I hope you enjoyed my book. I really can't wait to hear about how reading this book has helped you. Perhaps you have saved thousands of dollars because of one of my negotiation tips. Or maybe, after reading chapter 4, you've now managed to find a home you thought would have been out of your price range. Whatever your story is, I would genuinely love to hear it, and you can get in touch at **info@ pizzaandproperty.com**.

It's now time for you to pull your phone out of your pocket, and invite all of your mates around to your housewarming party. Congratulations, and have a drink for me!

THE LINGO

Certificate of currency. A document confirming your insurance policy is current. It should include details of the sums insured and the policy type and expiry date.

Chattel. An item of property that is generally not fixed to the land or building – such as furniture or appliances belonging to the homeowner.

Cooling-off period. A short period after committing to a home purchase where the buyer can change their mind. Cooling off works differently in each state and territory in Australia.

Due diligence. The investigation that a reasonable person is expected to take before entering into an agreement or contract.

Dutiable value. The value of the property that stamp duty is calculated on – either the price you paid for the property or its market value (whatever is greater).

Easement. A section of land that a third party has access to and the right to use for a specified purpose.

Encroachment. An intrusion on a person's territory, for example when a property owner violates the property rights of their neighbour by building or extending a structure to the neighbour's property or land.

Encumbrance. A restriction a third party may impose on your property. For example, a developer may have the right to tell you to build a fence that is 1.5 m tall within 12 months of moving in.

Exchange. Exchange of contracts. Once each party has signed the contract and a copy of the signed version is delivered to each party, the contract is exchanged. This is the trigger for the cooling-off period to begin in some states.

FHOG. First Home Owner Grant. A national scheme funded by the states and territories that awards a one-off grant to first home buyers who satisfy all the eligibility criteria.

Fiduciary duty. A commitment to act in the best interests of another person. Every selling agent in Australia has a fiduciary duty to their vendor, which must be upheld at all times.

Freehold property. A property title that the owner of the land owns forever.

Genuine savings. A term often used by lenders to describe savings you, yourself, have accumulated over a period of time, usually between three and six months.

Holding deposit. A sum of money that the selling agent may request from the buyer as part of an offer. It is used to signify how serious a buyer is about purchasing a property and is added to the home deposit once the contract has been exchanged.

LMI. Lenders mortgage insurance. An insurance payment that protects the lender if the borrower defaults on (fails to repay) their home loan.

LVR. Loan-to-value ratio. The ratio of your loan amount against the value of the property you are purchasing, calculated by dividing the loan amount by the value of the property.

Owners corporation (previously reviously known as body corporate). The legal entity that manages the common property of a housing development, for example gardens and lifts.

PPR. Principal place of residence. The property in which you reside, occupy and live that you regard as your home.

Pre-approval. When a lender has agreed on an amount that it is most likely willing to lend you based on the details you have provided of your financial situation.

'**Rent-vestor**'. Someone who purchases a property with the express intent of renting it out, then renting a separate dwelling to live in themselves.

Selling agent. The real estate agent who is selling the home on behalf of a vendor.

Sinking fund. Pool of money held by an owners corporation to pay for major repairs and maintenance on the common property.

Stamp duty. Tax the state and territory governments charge for certain property transactions.

Transaction eligibility threshold. The maximum price you are able to pay and still meet particular FHOG requirements.

Vendor. The person (or people) who currently owns and is disposing of the property (the seller).

ABOUT THE AUTHOR

Skateboarding and real estate may not seem like they have anything in common but, for Todd Sloan, one would not exist if it weren't for the other. If Todd had never picked up a skateboard as a kid, he's convinced he'd be dead or in prison. Being obsessed with skateboarding, he says, taught him more valuable lessons than he can count. He cites the resilience and persistence he had to learn through skateboarding as the catalyst for his success in real estate and business today. As a young skater, Todd learned to get up and try again every time he fell, which created a focus that may have gotten him into a little trouble – but mostly kept him out of it.

One might ask how a skateboarding-obsessed and arguably troublesome teenager would end up steadily climbing the ladder in the world of real estate, but Todd recognises that the former imparted some valuable lessons for the latter. The determination he learned from falling off that board time and time again aided him in reaching some colossal achievements, using his efforts to raise money for children's charities. In 2014, Todd walked over 800 km from Adelaide to Melbourne, with his steps counting towards a sizeable donation for CanTeen. Any average person would probably call it quits here, but Todd is not your average person. In 2016, he rode a pushbike over 3000 km from Darwin to Adelaide to raise money for HeartKids. Neither of these efforts came easy, but this never stopped Todd – he recognises that he had to go through a dark time and hit the bottom to learn that the only way to go from there was up.

Todd's passion for real estate has driven his journey as a property investor and renovator over the last decade. One of the only things he likes more than buying and selling real estate is talking real estate over pizza with good company. Enter 'Pizza and Property', Todd's weekly podcast that combines the worlds of real estate and tasty food with the good humour and insight that only he can bring.

These words might sound too good to be true, and perhaps a little biased – as if the author has written his own author's note, exaggerating his stories and triumphs. That's not the case here, though, as the person writing Todd's author's note is his little sister and as such, it is my duty to pull him down a peg or two – but he truly makes it easier said than done.

Pizza & Property podcast···

Find Pizza and Property on your favourite podcast app, or visit the website:

pizzaandproperty.com

ACKNOWLEDGEMENTS

There are so many people I know I should probably thank for making this book a reality. If I've forgotten you, please feel free to call me.

To everyone who helped by reading my drafts and giving their invaluably professional and personal insights, thank you. Thank you to Ainsley and Ben for making sure this book is factually in order and not just the ramblings of a madman who works in real estate. Thank you Peter and Chris for giving insights from your own specific professions. Thank you to both of my sisters for each giving me your spelling and grammar tips, and points of view. That means the world to me.

I'd like to thank my parents: Karine, and Bruce and Julie. Without your individual support, I would not be the person I am today. I would not have been able to create something like this. Thank you Mum, for giving me the ability to think differently and have the creative thoughts to make a project like this possible. Thank you Dad, for giving me the unstoppable confidence and work ethic to make my original thoughts into a reality. I grew up watching you work 60-hour weeks yet always finding time for me when I needed you (and to take me skateboarding). Thank you Julie, for always listening to me waffle on about one of my new ideas and being there to give me solid, straightforward advice that no-one else wants to tell me. You're all amazing people in your own ways, and I would not be the man I am today if it wasn't for the influence of each of you in my life.

Thank you Valerie: your belief in me at the beginning is one of the big reasons I even have the knowledge to write a book on this subject. Your fantastic work ethic, creativity and positive approach to life and business have been significant factors in making me into the real estate professional I am today. I am truly grateful you saw in me what I didn't see in myself.

Thank you to Lesley, Brooke and the whole team at Major Street: you all put up with more back-and-forth, variations, delays and stressed-out phone calls from me in the production of this book than I ever thought would happen. Your guidance will always be remembered – especially you, Lesley: taking the punt on publishing my book is something I will always be grateful for.

To my closest and dearest mates Ryan, Toddy, James and most of all Justin: you four have always been there for me since I can remember, through down times and the crazy fun times; especially you, Justin, my oldest and closest friend (more than James).

Most of all, thank you to my beautiful B! I really can't describe how lucky I am to have you in my life. Your constant support and encouragement of my never-ending rambling of ideas means the world to me. I'm so glad we met on that pyramid, even if Justin did almost die... I love you more than pizza Bianca, you're my girl. xx

REFERENCES

State and territory first home buyer schemes

Australian Capital Territory
revenue.act.gov.au/home-buyer-assistance

New South Wales
revenue.nsw.gov.au/grants-schemes

Northern Territory
nt.gov.au/property/home-owner-assistance

Queensland
www.qld.gov.au/housing/buying-owning-home/
financial-help-concessions

South Australia
revenuesa.sa.gov.au/FHOG

Tasmania
sro.tas.gov.au/first-home-owner

Victoria
sro.vic.gov.au/first-home-owner

Western Australia
www.wa.gov.au/organisation/department-of-finance/fhog

Chapter 1: Getting your finances sorted

The Property Nerds 2021, thepropertynerds.com.au.

Chapter 2: Free money?

Zahos, E 2020, 'The 10 most expensive cities around the world to buy property', Canstar, canstar.com.au/home-loans/expensive-cities-buy-property.

Chapter 6: What to expect when you're inspecting

Stults, R 2015, 'A Brief History of Opening Our Homes to Total Strangers (aka the Open House)', realtor.com, realtor.com/news/real-estate-news/brief-history-of-the-open-house.

Chapter 11: Settlement and moving in

Residential Settlements n.d., 'What is property settlement?', residentialsettlements.com.au/property-settlement.

INDEX

www.ingramcontent.com/pod-product-compliance
Lightning Source LLC
Chambersburg PA
CBHW031933190326
41519CB00007B/513